This book is ... ourne
or before th

THE BRITISH
IMMIGRATION COURTS

Other related titles from The Policy Press

Managing to survive: Asylum seekers, refugees and access to social housing
(1999) Roger Zetter and Martyn Pearl ISBN 1 86134 171 7 £14.99

*In search of a home: An evaluation of refugee housing advice and
development workers* (1998) Robin Means and Azra Sangster
ISBN 1 86134 095 8 £11.95

*Shifting spaces: Women, citizenship and migration within the
European Union* (1999) Louise Ackers ISBN 1 86134 038 9 £18.99 pbk;
ISBN 1 86134 127 X £45.00 hdbk

All the above titles are available from
Biblios Publishers' Distribution Services Ltd, Star Road,
Partridge Green, West Sussex RH13 8LD, UK
Telephone +44 (0)1403 710851, Fax +44 (0)1403 711143

THE BRITISH IMMIGRATION COURTS

A study of law and politics

Max Travers

The POLICY PRESS

First published in Great Britain in 1999 by

The Policy Press
University of Bristol
34 Tyndall's Park Road
Bristol BS8 1PY
UK

Tel   +44 (0)117 954 6800
Fax   +44 (0)117 973 7308
e-mail tpp@bristol.ac.uk
http://www.bristol.ac.uk/Publications/TPP

© The Policy Press, 1999
British Library Cataloguing in Publication Data
A catalogue record for this book is available from the British Library

ISBN 1 86134 172 5

Max Travers is Reader in Sociology at Buckinghamshire Chilterns University College, High Wycombe. His previous publications include *The reality of law* (Ashgate, 1997) and *Law in action*, edited with John Manzo (Ashgate, 1997)

Cover photograph © Stalingrad O'Neill. Demonstrator outside Oxford Crown Court during the trial of the 'Campsfield Nine', a group of West Africans charged with riot and violent disorder following a disturbance at Campsfield House Detention Centre in August 1997.

Cover design: Qube Design Associates, Bristol.
Printed and bound in Great Britain by Hobbs the Printers Ltd, Southampton.

Contents

v

Acknowledgements

This book reports the findings of a research project, funded by the Nuffield Foundation and the Economic and Social Research Council, which seeks to encourage debate about public policy relating to asylum and immigration in the United Kingdom.

I became interested in immigration control, entirely through serendipity, when my father was made a part-time adjudicator (an 'immigration judge'). Prior to his appointment, I had no idea that this court-system existed, nor of the large numbers employed in occupations and organisations concerned with immigration control. I also had no idea that so many people have a passionate opposition to controls, and have spent years campaigning against the policies of successive governments. I have tried to do justice to these different perspectives in this book, and hope that it will encourage others to conduct research about this area of public policy.

I would like to thank all the people who gave me access to research data, on behalf of a number of institutions. These include Keith Best, Shindo Maguire and Samina Kausar of the Immigration Advisory Service, Judge David Pearl and Jim Latter of the Immigration Appellate Authority, Ray Sams and Paul Stockton of the Lord Chancellor's Department, Geoff Brindle and Terry Neale of the Home Office, Alison Harvey who was then working for the Refugee Legal Centre, Mike Kaye of the Refugee Council, Sten Bronee who was then Deputy Director of the London office of the United Nations High Commissioner for Refugees, and Steve Cohen of the Greater Manchester Immigration Advice Unit, as well as the representatives and adjudicators in Thanet House and Hatton Cross who let me follow them around the courts, and found time to talk about the tasks and troubles of their working day.

I would also like to thank Dawn Pudney of The Policy Press and her team for their work, and my colleagues in the Department of Human Sciences at Buckinghamshire Chilterns University College for their support over a long period. I am particularly grateful to Rod Watson, Michael Lynch and Wil Coleman for their advice and suggestions.

Introduction

Immigration has been a contentious and controversial area of public policy in the United Kingdom since the Commonwealth Immigration Act ended most primary immigration in 1962. Community and political groups have campaigned against the restrictive policy of successive governments towards secondary immigration. More recently, Britain's treatment of asylum-seekers, as part of its obligations as a signatory of the 1951 United Nations Convention on Refugees, has also attracted a great deal of criticism.

The 1996 Asylum and Immigration Act which withdrew social security benefits from many seeking asylum in the United Kingdom, arguably produced greater moral outrage, among a broad spectrum of liberal opinion, than any other policy pursued by John Major's Conservative government. As this book goes to press, the 1999 Immigration and Asylum Bill will shortly receive its third reading in parliament, which will establish a system of cashless support for asylum-seekers in 'designated' accommodation around the country. Thousands have already demonstrated against Tony Blair's New Labour government which promised to restore full social security benefits to asylum-seekers, on humanitarian grounds, when it was campaigning for office in 1997.

One institution which has received some media attention during this period is the appeals system that reviews administrative decisions on immigration and asylum made by the British government. This was established for immigration decisions by the 1969 Immigration (Appeals) Act, following the recommendations of the Wilson Report, and has been administered by the Lord Chancellor's Department since 1987. Asylum-seekers were given a right of appeal by the 1993 Asylum and Immigration Act. This appeals system is technically an administrative tribunal – one of over 70 that have been established since the Franks Report of 1957 – but most people working there prefer to use the term 'court' which seems appropriate, given the formality of the proceedings, and the importance of the decisions being made for the lives of individual appellants[1].

My use of the term 'courts', rather than 'tribunals' in the title of this book should not, however, be taken as endorsing the perspective of practitioners. During my fieldwork, some adjudicators – the current name for the professional group making decisions in the courts – were lobbying to be allowed to use the title 'Immigration Judge' to acknowledge the technical character of their work. I later came to see this question of terminology in a different light when I interviewed civil servants in the Lord Chancellor's Department and the Home Office. At the risk of over-simplifying matters, some civil servants felt that they had failed over the years in preventing tribunals being 'taken over' by lawyers, since they had originally been intended as a cheap and informal means of resolving disputes between citizens and the state. This is an interesting example of how my research revealed different institutional perspectives on the courts, which raise general issues about the relationship between law and politics.

This book reports the findings of an ethnographic study of this court-system, which I conducted during the period February 1996 to June 1997. Most of the fieldwork was pursued in the courts at Hatton Cross near Heathrow airport, and at Thanet House in central London, although I also spoke to a range of people with a practical interest in immigration appeals, including a representative from the London Office of the United Nations High Commissioner for Refugees.

I have also taken an interest in the enactment of the Asylum and Immigration Acts in 1996 and 1999. I have attended meetings arranged by political groups and student societies opposed to the policies of successive governments, interviewed pressure groups and campaigning organisations, and followed debates in the media, and the House of Commons.

In contrast to the long list one often finds at the end of reports produced by pressure groups or management consultants, it will be apparent that this study is based on interviews with only a few people, working in some of the main organisations and occupations connected with the courts, and on the observation of only a small number of appeals hearings. This is partly the result of limited time and funding, but also owes much to my conviction, as a qualitative sociologist, that it is possible to learn a great deal from examining very small amounts of data, such as a single courtroom hearing, or one interview with a lawyer or civil servant.

My principal aim is to address a range of institutional and practical perspectives on immigration control through describing day-to-day work in different organisations. Chapters Four and Five look, in some detail, at the practical work of lawyers representing appellants and the Home Office, and of adjudicators (the judicial officials who decide the outcome of appeals) in the first tier of the immigration court-system. Chapters Six and Seven are a more general attempt to address the perspective of civil servants, and politicians, on the courts and immigration control.

The current preference in disciplines like sociology, law, cultural studies and political science is to write about these issues at a highly general or abstract level: to regard the detail of what happens in the courts, or the civil service, or in politics, as largely unimportant. My focus throughout will, however, be upon the practical concerns of people dealing with concrete tasks in particular institutional settings. This is a novel way of studying law and politics, and I hope will cause the reader to reflect upon the nature and effects of immigration control at both a human and institutional level.

There might be some objections to my focus on administrative agencies, rather than on the experience or perspective of appellants in the court-system. One critic complained that this was somewhat like studying a concentration camp from the guard's perspective, and that there was something immoral and objectionable about the whole enterprise. To meet this kind of concern, I have collected some additional data on appellants in asylum appeals, which raises particular methodological and interpretive problems, and plan to write a separate paper about this perspective on the appeals process. It might be added that I regard comparisons between the courts and concentration camps as unhelpful, in that there are obvious differences between the experience of asylum-seekers, and those who died in real concentration camps during the Second World War. I would also want to argue that it is necessary to understand the practical concerns of the people who work in the system, as well as the perspective of appellants, in order to make an informed political judgement about immigration control.

There are two bodies of sociological theory I will be drawing upon in this study of the immigration courts. The first is the fieldwork tradition in symbolic interactionism, and more specifically Everett Hughes' contribution to the sociology of work (1994). The symbolic interactionist commitment to ethnography and direct observation is best expressed by its most forceful advocate, Herbert Blumer, writing in the 1950s:

> ... the empirical social world consists of ongoing group life and one has to get close to this life to know what is going on in it. If one is going to respect the social world, one's problems, guiding conceptions, data, schemes of relationship, and ideas of interpretation have to be faithful to that empirical world. This is especially true in the case of human group life because of the persistent tendency of human beings in their collective life to build up separate worlds.... One merely has to think of the

> different worlds in the case of a military elite, the clergy of a
> church, modern city prostitutes, a peasant revolutionary body,
> professional politicians, slum dwellers, the directing management
> of a large industrial corporation, a gambling syndicate, a
> university faculty, and so on, endlessly.... To study [human
> beings] intelligently, one has to know these worlds, and to know
> the worlds one has to examine them closely. No theorising,
> however ingenious, and no observance of scientific protocol,
> however meticulous, are substitutes for developing a familiarity
> with what is actually going on in the sphere of life under study.
> (Blumer, 1969, pp 38-9)

Blumer was writing at a time when this kind of research was very much
a minority interest in an academy obsessed by grand theory and statistical
method, and, sadly, this remains the case today. There is, for example,
much of contemporary relevance in the following remark:

> Kudos in our fields today is gained primarily by devising a
> striking theory, or elaborating a grand theoretical system, or
> proposing a catchy scheme of analysis, or constructing a logically
> neat or elegant model, or cultivating and developing advanced
> statistical and mathematical techniques, or executing studies
> that are gems of research design, or ... engaging in brilliant
> speculative analysis of what is happening in some area of social
> life. To study through first hand observation what is actually
> happening in a given area of social life is given a subsidiary or
> peripheral position – it is spoken of as 'soft' science or journalism.
> (Blumer, 1969, p 38)

This study treats the immigration courts, and the making of immigration
policy more generally, as a set of interlocking social worlds that can *only*
be understood through direct observation, although interviews with
participants can reveal much about the activities and outlooks in different
occupational groups and organisations. It is, therefore, consistent,
empirically and theoretically, with Blumer's programme.

I will also be drawing upon the ideas of Everett Hughes, in looking at
the courts in later chapters, and particularly his insight that a comparative
perspective can reveal much of interest about work and organisations.
Hughes is famous for the observation that "the comparative student of
man's work learns about doctors by studying plumbers; and about

prostitutes by studying psychiatrists" (Hughes, 1994, p 79). The practical tasks and troubles encountered by advocates, judges and administrators in the immigration courts can similarly be compared to those experienced in other occupations; not least the problem, in a period of cut-backs in public services, of how to make best use of limited time and resources. Although there are important differences between the work of doctors and plumbers, the method used by Hughes – described by some commentators as the use of 'perspective by incongruity' – can reveal a human aspect to work which is not available to other approaches.

The second body of theory I will be using in this study is ethnomethodology, a field of sociology concerned with the interpretive and communicative methods used to display and make sense in social life. Ethnomethodologists in the studies-of-work tradition have investigated the practical content of work, and its reliance on technical and common-sense knowledge, through conducting ethnographies in a range of social settings (Lynch, 1993, Chapter 7). Researchers in the related tradition of conversation analysis have used discourse analytic methods to examine how language is used to perform a variety of occupational tasks (Drew and Heritage, 1992).

In an earlier study (Travers, 1997b), I described some features of work in a firm of criminal lawyers, drawing upon resources from the studies-of-work tradition. In this study, I will be using a similar approach to examine the immigration courts. This choice of an analytic framework was again partly dictated by practical considerations: I was unable to make tape-recordings of courtroom hearings or lawyer–client interviews during this project. I am also, however, committed to the view that the taken-for-granted skills and knowledge used in legal proceedings, which shape outcomes in the courts, are not available simply from looking at transcripts. It is also necessary to interview people about their day-to-day activities, and spend long periods of time in the field.

I begin in Chapter One with a selective review of academic literature from the sociology of racial and ethnic relations, which puts forward a case for the interpretive approach adopted in the rest of the book. The chapter also contains a brief history of attempts to restrict entry to the United Kingdom in the last 100 years.

Chapter Two describes the methods I used to research four social worlds whose members have a practical or personal interest in immigration appeals. These are the worlds of practitioners in the courts, civil servants, politicians and appellants. The chapter discusses my objectives and the problems I encountered in the project.

Chapter Three provides an overview of the appeals process. It introduces the main stages of decision making, the legal framework for appeals, and the occupational groups in the court-system. The 1999 Immigration and Asylum Act will result in some changes to this system, and I will be discussing how the structure of the courts, and the procedural rules which provide a framework for hearing appeals, have been understood as an administrative problem, and a political issue, in Chapters Six and Seven. Although this has been an area of rapid growth and development in English law, there have been no fundamental changes to the appeals system since 1969, and it will be substantially preserved by the 1999 Act.

Chapter Four looks at the practical work involved in determining primary purpose appeals. This rule, which operated from 1980, and was abolished when Labour came to power in May 1997, required immigrants, who wished to come to Britain on the basis of marriage, to prove that the primary purpose of the marriage was not to gain entry to the United Kingdom. It mainly affected members of the Asian community, seeking to bring in spouses from India or Pakistan through the arranged marriage system, as well as white British men seeking to marry women from the Third World. The focus of the chapter will be on how issues of law and evidence were understood by practitioners, both generally, and in the practical circumstances of particular appeals.

Chapter Five looks at the work of the courts in relation to asylum, focusing again on the legal and evidential issues in particular appeals. Since the late 1980s, there has been a great increase in the number of people claiming asylum in Britain as refugees from political persecution, under our obligations as a signatory of the 1951 United Nations Convention on Refugees. One question the chapter will address is the reason for the high refusal rate (96% of these appeals in 1996). Was this due to a 'culture of refusal' (the argument of political critics), or the fact that most asylum-seekers were 'bogus' (the argument of the Home Office)?

Chapter Six is mainly concerned with the perspective of the civil service in administering the court-system. There was a huge increase in the numbers seeking asylum in the late 1980s, and the courts did not have sufficient personnel or resources to keep up with the new appeals being referred by the Home Office. This chapter assesses a number of administrative and legislative measures taken by the civil service to address this problem, which include the 1996 and 1999 Immigration and Asylum Acts. I will particularly focus, however, on the routine work of the civil service which is often overlooked by political scientists. One section of the chapter looks at the work involved in drafting a new set of procedural rules in 1996, which illustrates how civil servants manage tensions between the executive and the judiciary.

Chapter Seven is concerned with the nature of immigration as a political issue, through looking at the work and perspectives of politicians, pressure groups and campaigners. The chapter looks at the history of immigration as an issue in post-war politics, and examines contributions to the parliamentary debates that took place during the enactment of the 1996 Asylum and Immigration Act. It also reviews the arguments put forward by academics and pressure groups for changing immigration policy in recent years.

The conclusion returns to the issue of perspectives, and considers the extent to which this interpretive approach represents an advance on more directly political contributions by academics to the sociology of racial and ethnic relations. I argue, following Max Weber, that the sociologist has a duty to respect the complex character of human group life, and to recognise the difficult, and sometimes intractable, nature of the problems faced by politicians and policy makers in any area of public policy. There are no easy answers to an issue like immigration control, but there is, perhaps, scope for a more generous response by Western governments.

Note

[1] Tribunal hearings were originally intended as informal occasions in which there would be no lawyers present. By this criterion, the immigration courts, and many other tribunals, have a distinctly court-like character. For a discussion of this issue, see Atkinson (1982).

ONE

Sociology and immigration

There is already a rich sociological literature that provides different ways of understanding immigration control, and can help us appreciate debates about this issue in social and political life. My objective in this chapter is to provide a selective review of the main approaches being pursued by British sociologists, but also to put forward a case for the interpretive approach adopted in the rest of this book.

The structure of the chapter will be as follows. I will begin with a short historical summary of immigration control in Britain, which is necessary to provide some context for the arguments of different sociologists. I will then review some of the main theoretical perspectives on immigration in the sociology of racial and ethnic relations, concentrating on the traditions of neo-Marxism and poststructuralism that currently dominate research and theorising in this field. In the second half of the chapter, I will identify a problem in this literature: the gap between the perspective of theorists and our everyday experience of the world. I will suggest that Robin Cohen's (1994) study of British policy towards asylum-seekers bridges this gap, through its focus on the actions and perspectives of government officials, pressure groups and politicians. This study takes this interpretive approach a step further by examining a range of institutional and practical perspectives in the immigration courts.

A short history of immigration control in Britain

Britain has experienced three waves of mass immigration in recent history. During the middle of the 19th century, the potato famine caused large numbers of Irish immigrants to come to Britain. The Censuses of 1841 and 1861 indicate an increase in those of Irish origin from 415,000 to almost 750,000. Towards the end of the century, political persecution, and later famine, and war, resulted in about 300,000 Russian Jews settling in Britain between the period 1870 and 1914 (Pollins, 1989), and they were joined by a smaller number of Jewish refugees from Germany prior to the Second World War. In the post-war period, Britain has experienced what one writer calls "nothing less than a rapid and quite unprecedented demographic and cultural transformation" (Spencer, 1997). Large numbers of citizens from Britain's ex-colonies in the Caribbean, the Indian subcontinent and Africa came seeking economic opportunities in the 1950s and 1960s, and have since brought over dependants, and raised families. The 1991 Census – which, like all statistics has to be treated critically as a source of data – found that about three million people described themselves as members of these ethnic groups in the United Kingdom: about 5½%, or one in 20 of the population, whereas they made up only 1% in 1940. The exact figures, given in Skellington (1996, p 57), are shown in Table 1.1.

Table 1.1: Population by ethnicity (1991)

Ethnicity	Number in 000s	% of total population	% of minority population
Black communities	890	1.6	29.5
African	212	0.4	7.0
Afro-Caribbean	678	1.2	22.5
South Asian communities	1,480	2.7	49.1
Bangladeshi	163	0.3	5.4
Indian	840	1.5	27.9
Pakistani	477	0.9	15.8
Other minority communities	645	1.2	21.4
Chinese	157	0.3	5.2
Asian	198	0.4	6.6
Various	290	0.5	9.6
All minorities	3,015	5.5	100.0
Majority communities	51,874	94.5	–

Source: OPCS (1991)

Estimates differ on future trends, and at what level the proportion of the population originating in the Caribbean, Asia and Africa is likely to stabilise, owing to the end of primary migration, and the effects of affluence on family size. An OPCS projection in 1979 estimated that it would be around 6% after the year 2000. Spencer (1997, p xii) suggests that "within another generation it is likely that Asian and black Britain will comprise about one tenth of the whole population".

Responses to immigration

Each of these three waves was accompanied by hostile public reaction to the newcomers, and by calls for immigration control (Holmes, 1991). There was widespread prejudice against the Irish, especially during the period of mass migration, and they were regularly portrayed as an inferior race, and as polluting the English national character (Holmes, 1991, p 16). Jewish immigrants were viewed by many as strange and unassimilable, and aroused hostility through competition for jobs and housing. An anti-semitic pamphlet by Joseph Banister in 1907, entitled *England under the Jews*, argued for controls on the grounds that immigrants brought down property values, and took British workers' jobs. It suggested that

> ... it is only a matter of time when the majority of the inhabitants of London and other large English towns will have as much right to be described as Anglo-Saxons as have the present mongrel inhabitants of the Hellenic kingdom to be called Greeks.
> (Banister, 1907) ANTÍ - semiul pamphlet

Migrants from Britain's ex-colonies in the Caribbean, Asia and Africa after the Second World War were also met by prejudice and hostility from sections of the public. There were incidents of racial violence in May and August 1948, and July 1949, in Birmingham, Liverpool, and Deptford (Layton-Henry, 1984, p 34). In the disturbance in Birmingham, a mob of between 100 and 250 white men surrounded and stoned a hostel housing Indian workers. There were two days of interracial violence in Camden Town in August 1954 (Glass, 1960). In August and September of 1958, there were more serious race riots lasting several days in Nottingham and Notting Hill involving large numbers of people. There were campaigns against immigration in Parliament, and Enoch Powell received immense public support for his speech delivered against the Race Relations Bill introduced by the Labour government in 1968 with the aim of combating discrimination in jobs and housing. Powell warned that:

> ... we must be mad, literally mad, as a nation, to be permitting the annual inflow of some 50,000 dependants who are, for the most part, the material of the future growth of the immigration descended population. It is like a nation busily engaged in heaping up its own funeral pyre. (Smithies and Fiddick, 1969, pp 35-43)

He concluded by predicting further violence: "As I look ahead, I am filled with foreboding. Like the Roman I seem to see the river Tiber foaming with much blood."

There were no restrictions imposed on the Irish, but a campaign against Jewish immigration resulted in the 1905 Aliens Act, which became the basis for later immigration controls. This Act refused entry to Jews without a means of support, and gave powers to the Home Secretary to deport 'undesirables', while establishing the principle that Britain would allow entry to those seeking refuge from political or religious persecution. Immigrants from the Caribbean, Asia and Africa after the Second World War were not aliens, but citizens of the United Kingdom and colonies under the 1948 British Nationality Act. This was a political move designed to preserve the British empire, and gave the right to any member of the empire or commonwealth, or any part of the empire that was subsequently granted independence, to live in Britain.

There are a number of historical versions of how immigration controls were established in 1948. Some accounts emphasise the need of the British economy for labour, and that there was a shift in policy when this was no longer required (Layton-Henry, 1984; Saggar, 1992). Others explain the imposition of controls as a result of governments responding to political factors. Spencer suggests that many politicians and civil servants favoured controls as early as 1945, but that the influence of the Foreign and Commonwealth Office prevented a change in policy until the early 1960s. The Commonwealth Immigration Act, enacted by the Conservative government in 1962, in response to a campaign for controls, restricted immigration from new members of the Commonwealth, through a system of vouchers designed to ensure that immigrants either had, or were likely to obtain, employment.

After initially opposing controls, the next Labour government went further with the 1968 Commonwealth Immigrants Act, an emergency measure that prevented East African Asians, who had become refugees as a consequence of the 'Africanisation' policy being pursued by Kenya, from coming to Britain. This established a patriality rule which restricted Commonwealth immigration to those with at least one parent or grandparent born in the United Kingdom. The effect of this Act, which attracted considerable criticism at the time, was to end coloured immigration from ex-colonies in the Caribbean, Asia and Africa, while imposing no restrictions on immigration from Canada, Australia and New Zealand.

The 1962 and 1968 Acts effectively ended primary immigration to

Britain, although it was the 1971 Immigration Act which established the system of control now in place. This gave the Home Secretary the power to make immigration rules which have since been amended several times to deal with new circumstances or strengthen controls. The system of appeals I will be examining in this book was established two years previously by the 1969 Immigration (Appeals) Act. Subsequent legislation in the 1980s – the 1981 British Nationality Act and the 1988 Immigration Act – closed some further potential loopholes, and made it easier to deport illegal immigrants. Secondary immigration was, however, still permitted under the immigration rules which allowed most of those who came during the 1950s and 1960s to be joined by their spouses and dependant relatives.

The importance of secondary migration

It is often believed that most immigration from the Caribbean, Asia and Africa took place before strict controls were established in 1968. Spencer, whose (1997) revisionist account might make uncomfortable reading for policy makers, suggests that immigration from the Caribbean peaked in the early 1960s, but that the bulk of immigration (both primary and secondary) from Asian and African countries took place during the late 1960s and 1970s, and was permitted under the controls established in 1962, 1968 and 1971. This was partly due to the humanitarian admission by Edward Heath's Conservative government in 1972 of 29,000 Ugandan Asians who had been expelled by Idi Amin. It was also due to steady secondary immigration during the 1970s. Spencer notes that:

At the beginning of the decade, the Asian and black population numbered some 1.2 million; the 1981 Census recorded an increase to 2.1 million. About a third of the increase can be accounted for by net immigration, which together with differential fertility rates, quite sharply changed the balance of the ethnic composition of black and Asian Britain. Inward movement from the Caribbean had already declined to below 5,000 a year by the end of the 1960s; during the 1970s it fell to negligible levels. On the other hand, inward movement of Indians (including East Africans) had increased sharply through the 1960s to reach a peak of over 25,000 in 1968. The year 1972 saw an exceptional immigration of close to 40,000, but the figure did not fall significantly below 20,000 for the rest of the

> decade. Pakistani migration also peaked in the 1970s rising to
> an average of close to 10,000 a year. The smaller communities,
> Bangladeshis, Chinese and Africans, all showed steady growth
> compared to the 1960s. The shift in the ethnic balance was
> remarkable. At the beginning of the 1970s the Caribbean
> community was comfortably the single largest component,
> making up about half of Asian and black Britain. By 1981, the
> Indian population had overtaken the Caribbean, and the total
> South Asian community was heading quickly for a figure double
> that of the West Indian community. (Spencer, 1997, p 146)

Secondary immigration became a political issue at the end of the 1970s,
when the immigration rules were amended with the aim of reducing the
number of Asians settling in Britain through arranged marriages. I will
be looking at the work of the immigration courts in deciding appeals
against decisions under the 'primary purpose' rule in Chapter Four. Most
people applying to settle in Britain from the Caribbean, Asia and Africa
are either married or engaged to British citizens, or wish to be reunited
with family members who came as migrant workers during the 1960s.
The vast majority of applications are granted by the Home Office without
the need for an appeal to the courts.

The asylum-seeker as a new source of immigration

Since the late 1980s, public debate about immigration has shifted to the
asylum-seekers who have arrived in increasing numbers, from a diverse
range of countries, seeking refugee status as part of Britain's obligations
as a signatory of the 1951 United Nations Convention on Refugees.

About 280,000 people claimed asylum in Britain in the period 1985–
97, an average of about 32,000 people each year since 1990. In recent
years, about 20% have been recognised as refugees or granted Exceptional
Leave to Remain (ELR) for temporary periods by the Home Office (see
Table 1.2). The remaining 80% have exercised their right of appeal, but
only a small percentage (4% in 1996) have been successful. However,
most unsuccessful appellants are not deported. Asylum-seekers, therefore,
represent another significant wave of immigration to Britain.

Table 1.2: Asylum applications (1985–97)

Year	Number of applicants	% given refugee status	% given ELR	% refused
1985	4,389	24	57	19
1986	4,266	13	70	17
1987	4,256	13	64	23
1988	3,998	25	59	16
1989	11,640	32	57	11
1990	26,205	26	60	14
1991	44,480	9	32	59
1992	24,605	3	37	60
1993	22,370	8	42	50
1994	32,830	5	20	75
1995	43,965	6	19	74
1996	29,640	7	15	77
1997	32,500	13	10	77

Source: *Home Office Statistical Bulletin* (Asylum Statistics 1997)

Immigration as a political topic

Immigration statistics, like statistics in general, are always, to some extent, incomplete and misleading, and can be interpreted in different ways, depending upon your political point of view[1]. Opponents of post-war black and Asian immigration have often warned of 'invasions' or 'swamping', and the threat to our indigenous culture and traditions[2]. It is sometimes suggested in this camp that there may be an additional two or three million illegal immigrants, and that our defences against immigration have been fatally weakened by our membership of the European Economic Community (EEC).

Those sympathetic to immigration emphasise the fact that blacks and Asians form only a fraction of the total numbers of post-war immigrants, or the number of immigrants in any one year, and that emigration always far exceeds immigration. A common charge is that the hostile reaction to immigration from the New Commonwealth is racist (in that there has been no outcry against white immigrants) and unjustified in economic terms since immigration benefits the country. The EEC, from this perspective, is often portrayed as having a policy of creating a 'Fortress

Europe', which will make it more difficult for coloured immigrants to settle in Britain[3].

The sociology of racial and ethnic relations

Debate about any topic in sociology usually revolves around a few recurring oppositions or themes, some concerned with epistemology, and others about the nature of society. If one group of theorists becomes dominant (and this is certainly the case for those writing about race and ethnicity in contemporary Britain), it will usually be claimed that these debates are no longer relevant, or have been supplanted by new ones internal to that paradigm, and textbook writers will seek to marginalise or forget the ideas and arguments of earlier theorists. However, orthodoxies in sociology seldom last for more than a generation (Sorokin, 1956), and ideas from previous paradigms have a habit of persisting in political debates outside the academy, even if they are neglected and marginalised in academic texts. For this reason, I will be presenting this review of the literature in terms of what some might consider an old-fashioned contrast between consensus and conflict traditions. Inside the academy, this criticism has some weight in that most theorising and research is now pursued using some variety of conflict theory. Outside the academy, however, political debates about immigration have not substantially changed since the 1960s, so it is important to understand and appreciate older perspectives.

The consensus–conflict debate revisited

I will begin by contrasting the approach of two theoretical traditions that represent alternative ways of understanding immigration control, and racial and ethnic relations more generally. The first tradition was founded by Robert Park in America during the early years of the 20th century: it viewed racial conflict and calls for segregation and immigration control as part of an inevitable series of stages towards integration and the eventual assimilation of ethnic and racial minorities in American society. The second tradition is that of British economistic Marxism in the late 1960s and 1970s. Sociologists and political economists writing in this tradition argued that immigration benefited economically dominant groups as a source of cheap labour, and gave employers an opportunity to divide and weaken the working class.

Robert Park and the race relations cycle

Robert Park is often considered to be the founder of the sociological study of racial and ethnic relations, and although he was writing in America in the first half of the 20th century, his work contains much of relevance for understanding debates about immigration control in post-war Britain[4].

Park was writing at a time of mass immigration into America from Europe and the Far East, and a mass internal migration to northern cities like Chicago by negroes from the rural South[5]. In Chicago, this migration led to growing social tensions arising from competition for scarce jobs, housing and social welfare. These culminated in a major race riot between negroes and whites in 1919, which resulted in 38 deaths, and large numbers being made homeless.

Many commentators at the time understood these developments in terms of the conceptual framework of Social Darwinism. It was widely believed in 19th-century Europe and America that racial prejudice had an evolutionary function to encourage diversity in the human species. It was pre-programmed into human beings biologically, so that the mixing together of races would inevitably lead to conflict (Banton, 1977). This meant that the only solution to the problems being experienced in Chicago was either immigration control, or racial segregation. These measures were advocated and justified on scientific grounds.

Park's significance for the study of racial and ethnic relations is that he was the first sociologist to challenge this biological understanding of racial prejudice. This still survives in the human sciences as sociobiology, which has enjoyed something of an intellectual revival in recent years in the form of 'Evolutionary Psychology', and as one version of rational choice theory, which asserts that there is a psychological inevitability to favouring members of your own group[6]. Separatist solutions are, today, most likely to be advocated by black nationalists, on the grounds that people in the Third World are innately superior to their white oppressors. There is equal evidence for both positions (*no* social scientific theory has, after all, ever conclusively been disproved) but beliefs about inherent racial prejudice are no longer widely held by most members of society.

Park explains that he was led to oppose Social Darwinism, and develop his own theoretical understanding of racial prejudice, through historical study. This amply demonstrated not simply that prejudice was not an inevitable feature of all human societies, but that the relations between racial and ethnic groups could change dramatically for the better over the course of time. One example Park liked to use was the relationship between African slaves and their masters in the Caribbean. Originally these were characterised by conflict – insurrections, escape attempts and the like – but over time, according to Park, a *modus vivendi* was established between the two groups. This is, in many ways, an unfortunate example, in that, even if one accepts there were less rebellions over time, this could be explained by the effects of brutal punishment and domination, rather than because of changes in biologically-based racial antipathy (the argument advanced by traditionalists in support of continuing segregation). Park, however, saw this, and other historical examples, as providing powerful evidence that the racial problems experienced by Chicago would gradually diminish over time; and they would do so without the need for any great programme of social intervention or engineering on the part of government.

Throughout his academic career, Park tried to distance himself from social policy initiatives, and establish sociology as a scientific discipline concerned with long-term social processes. He had little time for 'do-gooders', and disapproved of proposals made by Myrdal and other liberals in the 1940s for legal and educational measures to combat racial prejudice in the Deep South (Myrdal, 1944; Merton, 1976). On the other hand, many of his ideas did lend themselves to liberal initiatives designed to reduce prejudice: a good example of this is his concept of the 'race relations cycle' (Park, 1939) which was used as an analytic tool by Charles E. Johnson in his report on the Chicago riot of 1919, and by Bogardus (1959) in a study of problems arising from Japanese immigration to the west coast of America in the 1930s. Modified versions of the cycle were used by other students to explain the problems faced by negro migrants from the South in the 1930s and 1940s (for example, Frazier, 1957).

The basic idea informing these studies was that the experience of both immigrants and negro migrants in America could be understood in terms of a number of stages which will take place in any society where racial and ethnic groups meet.

Initial contact: Park suggested that migrants are often met with neutral curiosity when they arrive in a new country, and welcomed by employers as a source of cheap labour.

Competition: Before long, newcomers will start to compete with the indigenous population for scarce resources such as housing and jobs. Tensions will build up, leading to the growth of racial and ethnic prejudice, and self-segregation by different groups.

Conflict: This may, ultimately, result in a widespread breakdown in social order, such as the 1919 Chicago riot, graphically described by Faris (1948).

Accommodation: Over time, racial and ethnic tensions will subside, and groups will learn to coexist, while retaining separate communities, and marrying inside their own groups.

Assimilation: Park predicted that, eventually, immigrants will lose their sense of a distinct cultural identity, and be absorbed biologically into the indigenous population through intermarriage.

Park later qualified his ideas about the cycle to take account of the fact that not all historical contact between racial and ethnic groups would lead to assimilation (Driedger, 1996). Moreover, his students also doubted that negroes would be allowed to assimilate, given the prejudice they experienced in American society. E. Franklin Frazier believed that accommodation, rather than assimilation, would be the most likely outcome of contact between negroes and whites: they would live side by side in separate communities.

Park's ideas hardly amount to a developed theory, and need to be understood in the context of contemporary debates about immigration and racial difference in American society. Conservatives were either calling for immigration control, or urging immigrants to assimilate. President Wilson in 1915 spoke for this view:

> **You cannot dedicate yourself to America unless you become in every respect and with every purpose of your will thorough Americans. You cannot become thorough Americans if you think of yourself in groups. America does not consist of groups. A man who thinks of himself as belonging to a particular national group in America has not yet become an American, and the man who goes among you to trade upon your nationality is no worthy son to live under the Stars and Stripes. (Bouvier, 1992, p 11)**

Park, on the other hand, argued that maintaining a separate community as an ethnic group was necessary to enable immigrants to adjust to American life during the accommodation stage of the cycle, and was a precondition for eventual assimilation. This was also the case for negroes, who were required to develop a historical consciousness as a group, before they could become integrated into American society. Here, perhaps, Park has been least understood by critics in the conflict tradition. For him, conflict – in the form of race riots, competition for jobs and housing, racial attacks, and calls for immigration control – was an inevitable precondition for later improvements in racial and ethnic relations (Lal, 1990). Negroes could only improve their position through developing a sense of themselves as an ethnic group, with their own communal organisation and leadership that would secure economic and social benefits through competition with other groups. Racial and ethnic groups would, in this way, gradually absorb the cultural and economic values of American society, which would, in turn, become less prejudiced towards minority groups. Park believed that sociology had a role, along with journalism, in enabling the public to have an informed scientific understanding of these developments, and fostering tolerance during the inevitable periods of conflict.

Economistic Marxism and post-war immigration to Britain

A very different understanding of immigration control can be found in the work of economistic Marxists writing in Britain in the 1960s and 1970s. Their key assumption is that racial prejudice originated with capitalism during the 18th century, a set of social and economic relations based on the exploitation of labour. The migrants, who came to Britain and Europe after the Second World War, served the needs of capital as a source of cheap labour (Sivanandan, 1982). As a consequence, businessmen and politicians initially resisted calls for immigration control, while benefiting from internal divisions in the working class. Ultimately, it was expected that internal economic contradictions would lead to a political revolution, caused by the polarisation between capital and labour, which would result in a society no longer divided by race or class.

Castles and Kosack's (1973) *Immigrant workers and class structure* documents the position of immigrant groups in Western Europe as a pool of cheap labour doing mainly unskilled jobs. They begin their study by criticising writers in Britain, some of whom drew theoretical inspiration from Park, for viewing social problems arising from immigration in terms of 'race relations':

> **The race relations approach has dominated sociological research on immigration in Britain. The tendency has been to examine the problems of 'strangers' entering a 'host society', using the**

analytical categories of 'adaptation', 'integration', and 'assimilation'.... The problems connected with immigration are attributed partly to the immigrants' difficulties in adapting to the prevailing norms, and partly to the indigenous population's distrust of the newcomers who are distinguishable due to their skin colour. The problems can thus be reduced to the level of individual or small-group psychology, and can be solved by strategies which bring about a change in attitudes. The sociological study of immigration tends to degenerate into the more or less social-psychological examination of the 'colour' problem (or, for the liberal researcher, the 'white problem'). (Castles and Kosack, 1973, p 2)

The 'race relations' approach criticised in this passage had been developed by a group of British anthropologists and sociologists in the 1950s and 1960s. After initial optimism that coloured immigrants would be absorbed peacefully in the same way as the Irish[7], they became supporters of immigration control, but also of government measures to combat racism and discrimination. Castles and Kosack began their critique by suggesting that migrant workers in European countries experienced identical problems to blacks and Asians in Britain:

If that is the case, race and racialism cannot be regarded as the determinants of immigrants' social position. Instead, we shall argue, the basic determinant is the function which immigrants have in the socio-economic structure. (Castles and Kosack, 1973, p 2)

For Castles and Kosack, and other Marxist writers in this tradition, racial prejudice is always a direct product of class relations. The strategy for socialists should, therefore, be to educate all workers, whether black or white, about the real causes of their problems, with the aim of encouraging them to unite against the economically dominant ruling class. They observe, for example, that:

Workers who regard immigrants as inferior to themselves and who tacitly support their exploitation are victims of a false consciousness. Their behaviour is seriously detrimental to their own interests because it weakens the labour movement and reduces the political strength of the working class.... [The]

> false consciousness which gives rise to prejudice and
> discrimination will not be destroyed by humanitarian pleas. It
> can only disappear when it is supplanted not merely by a correct
> understanding of the position of immigrant workers, but by a
> class consciousness which reflects the position of all workers in
> society. (Castles and Kozack, 1973, p 482)

Educational initiatives, and anti-discrimination legislation were viewed as palliative measures addressed to symptoms, while Marxist theory provided a scientific analysis of the root causes of the problem.

The triumph of the conflict perspective

Very few academics in Britain would now subscribe to either the 'race relations' school, criticised by Castles and Kosack, or economistic Marxism, with its optimistic projection of a working-class revolution that would sweep away racial and class divisions. Instead, the approach that has become dominant – both institutionally in higher education, and also intellectually in the anti-racist movement – has been a heavily qualified form of Marxism that retains the belief that racism is a product of social and economic relations, while recognising the stability of capitalism. The analytic focus of neo-Marxist writers has shifted away from the economy towards studies of culture and politics. They now favour a short-term political strategy of promoting educational and legal initiatives to combat racism (see, for example, Cohen and Bains, 1988). Some still believe that global capitalism, the ultimate cause of racism, will eventually collapse, as Marx predicted, under the weight of its own economic contradictions[8]. Other left-wing academics have abandoned Marxist assumptions altogether, and have begun to pursue research programmes that are entirely concerned with culture, informed by poststructuralist ideas about discourse, identity and representation.

Two varieties of neo-Marxism

Neo-Marxist ideas are still immensely popular in British sociology, as well as internationally. They provide left-wing intellectuals with a set of ideas and concepts that enable them to retain the hope of an eventual radical transformation of society, during a period when there are arguably fewer prospects for progressive social change than at any time in the history of Marxism as a political movement. There are numerous varieties of neo-Marxist theory (Solomos, 1986), but it is worth contrasting two theorists who have influenced a great deal of academic writing about immigration and related issues.

Robert Miles and 'racialisation'

Perhaps the most important Marxist theorist during the last 30 years has been Louis Althusser who died in 1990. Althusser reworked the basic ideas of Marxism, so that, instead of conflicts between labour and capital determining changes in the rest of society, the economic, political and cultural spheres were viewed as autonomous parts of a social whole (Althusser, 1969). Whereas economistic Marxists had viewed change as arising from the contradiction between the economy and the rest of society, for Althusser, every part of society had its own internal tensions and contradictions, which in the right historical combination (or 'conjuncture'), could lead to change in the whole social system through an event like the Russian Revolution. There were also tensions and conflicts within classes, which he theorised not as homogeneous blocks, but as loose groupings of class 'fractions', which prevented the realisation of common economic interests (Poulantzas, 1975). Although there was little prospect of Marxists being successful in transforming society, given the stability of post-war capitalism, developments in the economy would eventually be 'determinant in the last instance' (a phrase first used by Engels). In the meantime, there was scope for Marxist political activity in the economic, political and cultural sphere.

Reading Robert Miles (1989, 1993), one is struck by the extent to which he is influenced by Althusser's ideas, although these are never made explicit in his writings on racial and ethnic relations, and one suspects he is closer to the economistic Marxists in seeing at least some possibility of class conflict leading to political change.

Althusser argued that our most basic ideas and categories were determined by the interaction of different structures in society, and in particular by what he called the 'Ideological State Apparatuses' of the educational system and the mass media. Miles, similarly, views ideas about racial difference as arising in particular historical circumstances, through a process of 'racialisation'. In his most recent book, he criticises writers in the economistic Marxist tradition for their use of 'race' as a category of analysis, although an outsider might have difficulty in distinguishing between the two positions. Perhaps the most important difference is that Miles places more weight on the interaction between economic, political and cultural factors, in explaining how people come to use ideas of 'race' in different historical periods.

Stuart Hall and cultural Marxism

According to both the economistic Marxists and Miles, the only effective political strategy for black and Asian immigrants would involve joining white workers in a common struggle against exploitation and discrimination. One reason why Stuart Hall's ideas about racial and ethnic relations have proved so popular in left-wing political circles is that they make it possible for blacks and Asians to organise their own campaigns against racism, while belonging to a progressive alliance of oppressed groups in society (Morley and Chen, 1996).

Contributors to *The empire strikes back* (Centre for Contemporary Cultural Studies, 1982), a collection influenced by Hall's ideas, acknowledged that there was no longer much hope for a political revolution, given the fragmentation of the working class (see also, Gilroy, 1987). They also challenged the view that non-class identities were ideological in character, a central feature of the writings of the economistic Marxists and Robert Miles.

Since then, other writers have argued that ethnicity, gender, and sexuality should also be treated as having a separate existence to class (see, for example, Anthias and Yuval-Davis, 1992), and a large literature has developed which explores the links between what are theorised as different dimensions of social subordination and oppression.

The rise of poststructuralism

The most recent developments in the sociology of racial and ethnic relations have involved a jettisoning of any remaining Marxist theoretical baggage, and an attempt to reconceptualise the study of racial and ethnic relations with a set of resources derived from poststructuralist writers such as Jacques Derrida and Michel Foucault (Rattansi, 1994).

These theorists still view society in terms of the conflict between dominant and subordinate groups, but offer few prescriptions for change. Instead, new research agendas have focused on Western representations of the Orient, building upon the work of Edward Said (1991), and on an appreciation of the complex character of ideas about 'race' and ethnicity in Western societies[9]. The emphasis is upon problematising the use of general categories such as 'class', 'race', 'gender' or 'ethnicity', while retaining a critical framework that emphasises the unequal power relationship between the West and the Third World.

This research agenda does have political implications, in that intellectuals in the 1970s and 1980s tended to use the term 'black' indiscriminately to refer to a wide range of ethnic and racial groups[10]. It also represents, to some extent, a return to viewing 'ethnicity' rather than 'race' as a central problematic, in that British researchers are starting to acknowledge the need for more research on the culture and history of different groups. Many empirical studies of ethnicity had been conducted during the 1950s and 1960s by anthropologists (Banks, 1996), but these were criticised by Marxists and neo-Marxists for supporting the assumptions of the 'race relations' school. It is now recognised that "in making the conceptualisation of racism a priority", critics "failed to develop a theoretical framework for an elaborated analysis of wider social and cultural processes" (Solomos and Back, 1996, p 11).

The most recent theoretical statements influenced by poststructuralist ideas emphasise the way in which ethnic groups, or 'diasporas', maintain their own cultural cohesion, but also develop 'hybrid' identities in a multicultural society, effectively an endorsement of Park's ideas concerning the accommodation stage of the race relations cycle (Spivak, 1987; Bhabha, 1994). One ethnographic study, influenced by these ideas, almost amounts to a celebration of cultural mixing and assimilation between young people from different ethnic backgrounds, with little emphasis on racism and discrimination (Back, 1996).

The continuing relevance of the consensus tradition

Although neo-Marxists and poststructuralists currently dominate discussion about racial and ethnic relations in the academy, assumptions derived from the consensus tradition continue to underpin discussions about this issue in political life and the media. The widespread condemnation of the police, and 'institutionalised racism', following the publication of the (1999) Macpherson Report, which investigated the failure of the Metropolitan Police to secure convictions after the racially-motivated murder of Stephen Lawrence, was wholly confined within these assumptions. No commentator suggested that unemployment or bad housing might be responsible for creating or aggravating racial prejudice in South London.

The same assumptions continue to underpin a political consensus supporting immigration control in Britain. Park was an opponent of controls in America, but the 'race relations' school in Britain came to support them as a means of alleviating the problems that arose during the competition and conflict stage of the race relations cycle. Successive governments have pursued a policy of maintaining 'firm but fair' immigration control, while pursuing educational and legal initiatives intended to combat racism.

It can also be suggested that, if one looks behind the political rhetoric, much writing by conflict theorists is also premised on similar assumptions, now that there is no longer a belief in the prospect of a working-class revolution. Few sociologists have written explicitly about immigration policy since Castles and Kosack and Sivanandan; but I suspect that most neo-Marxist or poststructuralist theorists writing in this field would accept the need for some form of control. They would, however, understand this as the product or symbol of unequal power relations (for example, as a legacy of Western imperial dominance), rather than as a pragmatic measure to maintain good 'race relations'.

A problem in the literature: the gap between the perspective of theorists and everyday experience

A common criticism of neo-Marxist and poststructuralist writing on racial and ethnic relations is that it is remorselessly abstract in character. Texts by neo-Marxists like Miles, Hall and Gilroy, or poststructuralists like Rattansi and Bhabha, usually take the form of commentaries on other neo-Marxist and poststructuralist theorists, or political/philosophical reflections directed at an audience of fellow intellectuals, with few concessions to the general reader. One rarely gets a sense of how members of different racial and ethnic groups understand their place in British society.

Here, for example, is an extract from *The empire strikes back*, which discusses the relationship between race and class:

> **Although ... we see race as a means through which other relations are secured or experienced, this does not mean that we view it as operating merely as a mechanism to express essentially non-racial contradictions and struggles in racial terms. These expressive aspects must be recognised, but race must also be approached in its autonomous effectivity. (Centre for Contemporary Cultural Studies, 1982, p 11)**

This kind of analysis does not address the day-to-day experiences of members of racial and ethnic groups, or how they understand their prospects and problems in British society. Instead, it puts members of these groups into the broad categories of 'race' and 'class', and then discusses problems arising from how the relationship between the two categories have been understood within Marxist theory. This is done using a theoretically-dense, technical language which students are taught to use when they take courses in sociology and cultural studies in higher education, but cannot easily be understood without this specialised training.

Poststructuralists fare little better, from this perspective, despite their aim to improve upon the categories used by Marxists. Rattansi describes one research strategy in the following terms:

> ... the first ... move must be to decentre and de-essentialise, by postulating what is often glimpsed but rarely acknowledged and accepted with any degree of comfort: that there are no unambiguous, water-tight, definitions to be had of ethnicity, racism and the myriad terms in-between.... Indeed, all these terms are permanently 'in-between', caught in the impossibility of fixity and essentialisation.... One programmatic conclusion would be.... to eschew tight definitions, and instead to engage in Foucauldian genealogical and archeological projects, exploring the accretion of meanings, political affiliations, subject positions, forms of address, regimes of truth and disciplinary practices involved in the construction of particular myths of origin, narratives of evolution and forms of boundary-marking and policing engaged in by different 'communities' in particular historical contexts. (Rattansi, 1994, p 53)

This is an interesting passage in that it illustrates both the possibilities, and limitations in poststructuralist theorising. The first part of the extract is addressed to the problems faced by theorists in trying to secure an empirical purchase upon social reality. Analytic categories like 'race', 'ethnicity', 'racism' and 'class' will never reflect the full complexity of social relationships on the ground.

This might suggest the need for studies that address how members of society understand categories such as 'racism', 'ethnicity' and 'all the myriad terms in-between', in an attempt to bridge the gap between theory and the social world. Rattansi, however, envisages a programme in which ideas and concepts from another theorist, in this case Foucault, are used to describe the world, in a way that is even further removed from the way we normally understand our own activities. The perspective of everyday experience is again subordinated to the perspective of the theorist.

Bridging the gap between theory and the everyday world

The root of this problem arguably lies in the fact that the kind of theorising pursued by neo–Marxists and poststructuralists is openly competitive towards the understandings, and epistemological assumptions, of social actors (see Prus, 1996, Chapter 7). Sociologists in this tradition tend to present themselves as having a superior insight into the structure of society than ordinary members of society. This means that there is always a potential tension between their accounts, and what Schutz (1973) terms the 'natural attitude': the way we understand the world in our ordinary, everyday lives[11].

There is, however, an alternative way of thinking in sociology, known as the 'interpretive' or 'action' tradition, that adopts a non–competitive or non–ironic stance towards the perspective of social actors. The aim here is not to construct a body of theory – neo-Marxist, poststructuralist, or whatever – to explain people's actions, but to explicate how social actors understand their own activities. This approach originates out of 19th-century debates about core issues in the discipline, and, in particular the methodological writings of Max Weber (1949, 1979), who argued that sociology should be concerned with the study of meaningful social action.

Interpretive approaches have become increasingly influential in sociology in recent years, both in their own right, and through being absorbed and assimilated into mainstream 'structural' traditions, and have informed a great deal of theorising and research in different sub-fields of the discipline. They have not so far, however, had a significant impact on the sociology of racial and ethnic relations, or social stratification more generally. This book will demonstrate one way in which interpretive sociologists can contribute to the study of racial and ethnic relations, although there are many other topics that could be addressed from this theoretical perspective.

At this point, it might be added that, for interpretive sociologists, the manner in which social actors understand categories like class, gender and race is treated as the central analytic topic, so that all of them should, strictly speaking, be placed in inverted commas (or 'phenomenological brackets'). Because, however, any category can be treated in this way, it makes equal sense to omit the brackets, which is why I have been using the category race without quotation marks.

This is also intended to encourage reflection about the way we use categories as sociologists. After all, the reason why it has become customary in British sociology to use quotation marks around the word race, although never around the word class, is because of the continuing, albeit usually unacknowledged, influence of Marxism. A central theme in the work of Marxists and neo-Marxists, such as Robert Miles, has always been the insistence that 'race', 'ethnicity' and 'nation' (to follow his use of quotation marks) are false beliefs, which are ultimately caused by capitalism, whereas class, as understood by the theorist, but not necessarily in the same way by the social actor, is an *objective* reality. From an interpretive perspective, on the other hand, there can be no such thing as a false belief; but how social actors actually use concepts like race or ethnicity in everyday life may be a complex matter that requires careful study.

A recent Weberian study

There are many varieties of interpretive sociology, some of which go further than others in their focus on the perspective of social actors. A good example of a study about immigration control, informed by a Weberian interest in meaning and action, is Robin Cohen's (1994) *Frontiers of identity*.

This presents an overview of British policy towards outsiders, focusing on how politicians and civil servants have supported a tough policy in detaining and deporting illegal immigrants, and tried to prevent asylum-seekers coming to Britain. It also examines the activities of pressure groups and campaigners, particularly in the churches, in campaigning against deportations through the sanctuary movement during the 1980s.

In marked contrast to the approach of neo-Marxist and poststructuralist theorists, Cohen suggests that sociologists should study the actual processes involved in constructing national boundaries. He notes that:

> ... there are real agencies and agents involved in the management of the processes of acceptance and rejection of 'the Other': the 'frontier guards', so to speak, of the national identity. These frontier guards include everyone from immigration officers and judges to newspaper editors, Home Office ministers and other politicians, as well as social and political movements that seek

> to influence the ideological and legal parameters of nationality,
> citizenship and belonging. Again, there are real policies,
> structures and institutions that constrain the frontier guards'
> and their victims' freedom of action, and real changes in the
> way these actors, policies, and structures have interacted over
> time. (Cohen, 1994, p 2)

It should be evident, even from this extract, that Cohen's political views
heavily colour his account, which prevents him from fully addressing the
perspectives of either 'frontier guards' or their 'victims'. He is, for example,
highly critical of the Immigration Service and the Home Office, who
"are working with narrow or outdated outlooks, and secretly bending
the will of parliament to their own preferences" (Cohen, 1994, p 210);
but he provides very little detail about the work of immigration officers,
or civil servants, or the constraints on their freedom of action. Nevertheless,
despite this shortcoming, the book demonstrates what can be achieved
by adopting a sociological perspective which is sensitive to meaning and
action.

The potential contribution of the interpretive tradition

My aim in this study is to address the topic of immigration control, in a
way that goes further than Cohen, in addressing how social actors
understand their own activities. To do so, I will be drawing upon resources
from symbolic interactionism and ethnomethodology, two approaches to
studying social life which form part of the interpretive tradition.

It must be acknowledged, to begin with, that very few sociologists in
this tradition have been concerned with the study of racial and ethnic
relations, or immigration control[12]. This is, therefore, to some extent, a
pioneering study, intended to open up avenues for empirical investigation,
as well as to explore the theoretical implications of these approaches for
the academic study of law and politics. There are, however, many studies
by symbolic interactionists and ethnomethodologists that show what can
be achieved in investigating similar topics.

Symbolic interactionism, which is the larger and older of the two
traditions, with its roots in the pragmatist tradition in American philosophy,
has always addressed social issues and problems, as well as pursuing a
scientific agenda in studying society (Prus, 1996, 1997; see also Cooley,
1918). The central objective of symbolic interactionist research is to
address how human beings find the world around them meaningful in

their everyday lives. The researcher should ideally spend a long period of time in close contact with the members of a particular social setting, community or occupational group, with the aim of obtaining an 'intimate familiarity' with their practical concerns and problems. A classic symbolic interactionist study about racial and ethnic relations is Liebow's *Tally's corner* (1967), which was based on a year's fieldwork among a group of street-corner men in a black ghetto in Washington during the 1960s, and supplies a sensitive and insightful account of their perspective towards employment, women and family life.

Interactionists in Britain have been much criticised by structural sociologists, and especially Marxists, for focusing on the 'micro' level of society, while neglecting the social structures which shape and constrain the actions of individuals. McBarnet (1981), for example, has noted that interactionist studies of law reveal how the actions of the police often fall short of legal ideals, but do not address how laws are made, or their role in reproducing and maintaining capitalism. The more diverse American literature, however, has always been less vulnerable to this criticism. There have been some important studies about how laws are made (Becker, 1963; Gusfield, 1966), and the political processes in government organisations and bureaucracies (Selznik, 1966; Katz, 1982), alongside ethnographic studies of enforcement. There are, therefore, precedents for my own interest in the perspective of civil servants, and politicians, as well as practitioners and appellants in the immigration courts.

Ethnomethodology is a research tradition that goes further than symbolic interactionism in studying the detail of everyday human practices (Heritage, 1984; Sharrock and Anderson, 1986). A central argument has been that a whole domain of activities has been largely ignored by other traditions. Ethnomethodological studies have demonstrated that there are countless phenomena in the social world, ranging from the skills used in ordinary conversation, to the practical content of technical activities, which have not so far been investigated, or taken seriously, by sociology. In turning their back on the 'big' topics studied by other sociologists, and focusing on the mundane, ethnomethodologists have, in effect, been making a political point about what the discipline should be doing, if it has pretensions to be concerned with the scientific study of society.

There is, however, no reason why ethnomethodologists cannot address any substantive topic studied by other sociologists. There have, as yet, been no ethnomethodological studies on the legislative process, but a number of researchers have gone further than symbolic interactionists in investigating how decisions are made inside law-enforcement and other government agencies[13]. Three of the best known are Cicourel's (1968) study of decision making in the apprehension and charging of juvenile delinquents in two American cities, Cicourel and Kitsuse's (1963) study of the work of school counsellors, and Sudnow's (1965) study of the work of public defenders. Each raises political questions about the fairness of these institutions through describing the content of routine day-to-day work, and illustrates how ethnomethodology can contribute to our understanding of public issues and social problems.

Although they differ considerably in the way they conceptualise meaning and action, symbolic interactionism and ethnomethodology have much in common when contrasted to the mainstream sociological literatures reviewed in this chapter. In contrast to structural traditions in the discipline, they each view human beings as active, interpreting agents, who produce social structures through their actions. The emphasis is on studying how people reflect, and act, in the situations and contexts in which they find themselves; rather than on their relationship to wider social structures and processes, whether these are theorised as 'late–modern capitalism', 'risk society', 'regimes of truth', 'the unconscious', 'globalisation', 'governmentality', or any of the other popular abstractions used to explain human actions in the contemporary social sciences.

In terms of research practice, they are each committed to naturalistic methods of investigation: to getting close to human beings, as they live their lives in particular social settings, and attempting to describe what they do, in a way which remains faithful to how people understand their day–to–day activities in those settings.

In the best studies, this is done in a simple, matter-of-fact way, which attempts to describe and record the talk and actions of people going about their business in everyday situations. There is a suspicion both of sociological theorising (when this results in the views and opinions of ordinary members of society being subordinated to those of the analyst), and also of methodology, in the sense of the standardised body of procedures that sociologists are required to follow, if they wish to produce findings that are taken seriously by other members of the discipline.

Blumer suggests, for example, that there are all kinds of techniques one can use in pursuing an interpretive study, which include "direct observation, field study, participant observation, case study, interviewing, use of life histories, use of letters and diaries, use of public documents [and] panel discussions" (1969, p 50). If he was writing today, the list would, no doubt, also include popular qualitative research methodologies, such as 'grounded theory' or 'conversation analysis'. However, Blumer also suggests that there are dangers in allowing any research method to acquire 'a standardised format'. Instead, they should be viewed simply as "instruments for discovering what is taking place in human group life" (Blumer, 1969, p 50).

My objectives in studying the immigration courts

The research methods I have used in this study reflect a commitment to the interpretive tradition, and an interest in the research questions pursued by symbolic interactionists and ethnomethodologists. In studying the immigration courts in this way, I hope to show that there are alternatives to the dominant paradigms of neo–Marxism and poststructuralism that can be used in studying racial and ethnic relations[14].

I would also like to feel that my approach to this topic has considerable implications beyond the study of racial and ethnic relations. For one thing, in addressing the perspectives of lawyers, civil servants and politicians (admittedly in different degrees of depth), this study can also be viewed as an interpretive contribution to the sociology of law and politics.

More generally, I hope to show that it is possible to contribute to debates about political and moral problems by addressing how people understand their own day-to-day actions. Interpretive sociologists are often criticised for being apolitical, or for neglecting wider social structural forces in their attention to the 'actors' point of view' in particular social settings. In fact, I hope to show that it is only through examining how social actors understand their practical problems in particular social settings (ranging from practitioners in the courts to government ministers) that one can make an informed judgement about immigration control as a political issue.

Notes

[1] For an analysis of the production of immigration statistics in Europe, see Barbesino and Singleton (1995).

[2] One recent example is the speech made by Norman Tebbit at a fringe meeting of the 1997 Conservative Party conference about the dangers for traditional British values and culture posed by the rise of a multicultural society.

[3] There has been a lot of academic interest in the development of a coordinated system of controls throughout Europe, as a result of the 1990 Dublin and Schengen intergovernmental agreements. See, for example, Bunyan (1991), Webber (1993) and Joly (1996).

[4] For an overview of this tradition, and Park's ideas about racial and ethnic relations, see Lal (1990), Persons (1987) and Wacker (1995).

[5] The term 'negro' was first used in this period by members of the liberal intelligentsia, like Park, as an attempt to replace less polite ways of referring to the descendants of the African slaves who had been brought to America in the 18th century. By the 1960s, 'negro' itself had become a perjorative term, and black power groups encouraged their members, and supporters, to use the term 'black'. Today, the preferred term used by liberals is 'African American'. In Britain, the term 'black' is still widely used, although academics have always been conscious about how difficult it is to describe members of different ethnic and racial groups without giving offence (Mason, 1990). Remarkably, there has been very little research on how people themselves use racial and ethnic categories in the course of their day-to-day lives (although, see Hughes and Hughes, 1981).

[6] See Van den Berghe (1981) for an example of a sociobiological explanation for racial prejudice, and Hechter (1987) for a review of rational-choice theories in psychology. The renewed popularity of sociobiology can be explained by the fact that prejudice remains stubbornly present in most societies, despite every effort made to eradicate it through educational programmes or legal sanctions. The strongest argument for sociobiological over sociological explanations would, of course, be if someone succeeded in identifying the gene responsible for causing racial prejudice.

[7] A good example of a British study influenced by Park is Sheila Patterson's (1965) *Dark strangers*. This describes the difficulties faced by West Indians in Brixton in the late 1950s, at what Park would describe as the competition stage of the cycle. Patterson predicted that, like previous groups of immigrants, they would eventually become assimilated, and be 'biologically absorbed' into the rest of the population.

[8] Much of the current wave of sociological writing about 'globalisation' – the set of interconnected economic, political and cultural developments which is creating a more unified world society – is written by intellectuals who are still hopeful that it will eventually lead to the transformation of human life in the way Marx

predicted. See, for example, Lash and Urry (1987, 1993) and Giddens (1990) who emphasise the contradictions built into the world economy, and the problems of a society based on affluence, and over-production, while recognising the stability of capitalism. This kind of macro-theorising, which owes much to the ideas of classical theorists of modernity such as Marx, Durkheim and Weber, has little directly to say about racial and ethnic relations. Some texts advance a similar line to Robert Park in suggesting that there will be an increased mixing of cultures and peoples: a kind of American 'melting pot' on a global scale (Cornell and Hartmann, 1997).

[9] This field has become known as post-colonial studies and has, to some extent, replaced the sociology of racial and ethnic relations in many universities and colleges (see, for example, Ashcroft et al, 1995). It is almost exclusively concerned with the study of literature, and different varieties of poststructuralist theory, rather than the empirical study of social processes.

[10] It has recently become accepted that the term 'black' should be abandoned, following the critiques made by Modood (1992) and Hall (1989), and by collections like Donald and Rattansi (1992), since it fails to distinguish between 'Afro-Caribbeans' and 'Asians', or between subgroups within these categories. It is still, however, widely used in undergraduate essays.

[11] Scholars working in this tradition rarely acknowledge that their interpretation of social reality is far removed from that held by ordinary members of the cultures they are studying. Back, however, in the introduction to his (1996) ethnographic study about minority youth cultures, notes that he has been surprised by "the degree of resistance among my students regarding this new cultural politics", which most of them see as "the utopian musings of an older generation of critics who have lost touch with the very cultures they claim to interpret".

[12] One exception is Janet Gilboy (1991) who has examined how decisions are made by immigration inspectors at an American airport using ethnographic methods. She spent 102 days observing their work, and conducted informal interviews with 36 inspectors, mainly by taking advantage of the 'dead time' between flights.

[13] Hester and Eglin (1992, pp 71–2) note that "the central phenomenon of ethnomethodological interest ... is the intelligibility of the constituent activities through which ... law is made". These include the "claims-making activities" of pressure groups and politicians, "the work of legislative assemblies and their

committees", and "judges' interpretations and applications of statute and case-law". They also argue that "for ethnomethodology, law is 'made' whenever 'law' is invoked or otherwise used, that is, in the ordinary work of courtroom prosecutions and police apprehensions".

[14] For a review of work in this field, see Bulmer and Solomos (1999).

TWO

Researching a court-system

This chapter describes the methodological problems I encountered in studying four groups of people who have a practical interest in the immigration courts: legal practitioners; civil servants; politicians; and appellants. Each of these groups has a public face, so it is possible to learn a great deal about legal proceedings, or appellants, from sitting at the back of courtrooms; about the work of civil servants from the annual reports of government departments; and about immigration as a political issue through attending public meetings or watching debates in parliament. They can also, however, be understood as private social worlds, whose members have a distinctive viewpoint on the appeals process, which is not immediately available to outsiders.

Understanding the private world of the courtroom

There is a large sociological literature about the courtroom, which can be explained by the fact that courts offer a rich source of publicly-available data about most aspects of society. In America, and some European countries, researchers can usually obtain permission to make audio- or video-recordings of courtroom hearings, and important cases, such as the Kennedy Smith rape trial, and the O.J. Simpson murder trial, are publicly available on television[1]. In Britain, it is not normally possible to make audio- or video-recordings of criminal or civil hearings, but anyone can sit at the back of a courtroom and take a full set of notes.

The immigration courts as a public institution

There are immigration courts in a number of cities in Britain, and anyone is entitled to observe appeal hearings. The first court I visited was in Manchester. This is situated on the third floor of an office block in the city centre, which is also used by the Department of Health and Social Security. The hearing rooms in this building have been converted from offices. Tables have been arranged to form a courtroom in which the representatives for the appellant and the Home Office (in court slang,

'HOPOs') sit on opposite sides of the room facing the adjudicator. Appellants give their evidence between the two representatives, often accompanied by an interpreter (see Figure 2.1).

Figure 2.1: Layout of hearing rooms

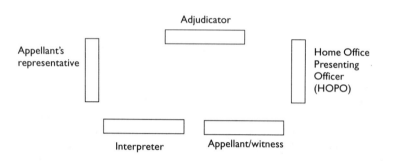

I also spent a few days at the hearing centre at Wood Green, a setting already known to sociologists from Paul Rock's (1993) ethnographic study of the same building when it was a crown court (which is now based in the impressive *palais de justice* next door). According to Rock, practitioners in this building used to describe it as 'the bunker'. It contains several large old-fashioned hearing rooms with bad acoustics, in which the judge sits on a high platform looking down on the court. Each room also contains a dock for the defendant, with a separate entrance to the cells. In the immigration appeals I observed, the adjudicator entered through a side-door, and sat in the judge's chair. Appellants gave evidence from the front of the court, but did not use the raised platform that would have been used by witnesses when Wood Green was a crown court.

I conducted most of the fieldwork in the two courts which were closest to my home near High Wycombe in Buckinghamshire. The main immigration court in central London in 1996 was Thanet House, whose main entrance was a doorway between an Italian sandwich bar and the Wig and Pen club, almost directly opposite the main entrance to the Royal Courts of Justice on the Strand. Inside, this was much like the Manchester courts, in that appeal hearings took place in converted offices[2].

I spent most time observing hearings in Hatton Cross, the largest hearing centre in the country, which contains 20 courtrooms. It is a modern, three-storey building, situated on an industrial estate near Heathrow airport, next to the headquarters of the delivery firm DHL.

There are spaces for about 100 cars around the building, which are generally full by the time the courts start sitting at 10.00 am. The only indication that it is a court are the words 'Immigration Appellate Authority' above the main entrance, and a caged area at the back of the building for receiving detainees.

Inside, the building feels and looks much like a court of law, although the hearing rooms are smaller than those at Wood Green. In contrast to the courts in Manchester, each contains a raised platform for the adjudicator, who sits beneath the Royal Coat of Arms[3]. There is also a separate entrance for adjudicators in most hearing rooms.

All these courts are open to the public, and there are spaces for between 10, and in some cases 20 people, to sit at the back of hearing rooms. On one occasion, I met a staff reporter from *The Times*, who had been told to cover a particular appeal because *The Guardian* had ran a story about it the previous day[4]. I was, however, usually the only outsider present, which became an issue on two occasions, when the appellants instructed their representatives to find out why I was taking notes[5]. Political dissidents often wish to conceal their whereabouts, and the fact that they are applying for asylum, from their own governments. When they learnt that I was a British academic, and had no connection with the secret police in their own countries, they were happy to proceed with their evidence.

Appeals hearings as a methodological problem

The public side of legal proceedings that can be observed, and recorded, in the courtroom has provided a rich source of data for a number of sociological and sociolinguistic traditions. Conversation analysts have used tape-recordings to examine the properties of courts as speech-exchange systems, and the communicative and interpretive skills employed by lawyers and witnesses (for example, Atkinson and Drew, 1979; Matoesian, 1993; Komter, 1997). Ethnomethodologists have focused on the public observability of courtroom hearings (Lynch, 1997), and on their character as self-explicating settings (Pollner, 1974), in which court-users learn how to act from observing how judges dispose of prior cases. Sociolinguists have also used transcripts from trials to make political points about the role of law in society: how law and legal procedure operates against racial and ethnic minorities, women or the working class (for example, O'Barr, 1982; Levi and Walker, 1990; Conley and O'Barr, 1998).

All these approaches have produced valuable findings, but what they do not address is how events in the courtroom are understood by participants during any particular hearing. While anyone can get access to the public face of the immigration courts by sitting at the back of appeals hearings, there is also a private dimension to the work of adjudicators and representatives that is considerably more difficult to research.

I explored some aspects of this methodological issue in an earlier study, as a problem raised by the American sociologist Harold Garfinkel, when he observed that the sociology of work tells us little about the content of everyday, occupational activities (Travers, 1997b, Chapters 1-2). From another disciplinary perspective, legal theorists have often complained that sociology cannot address the technical content of legal practice, and that this is a fundamental weakness in the sociology of law. Bannakar (1997) has observed that:

> ...jurists ... describe their resentment and dislike of sociological intrusions and trespassings, not so much because they are afraid of disclosures, but because the sociologist is an outsider who does not grasp the intricate meaning of what they do. The fact that every sociologist can probably understand every word used in an Act or a legal decision, does not necessarily mean that he/she can interpret the Act or the legal decision in a legally correct fashion or even realise its legal significance or implications. Then, the sociologist, who cannot understand what is actually happening from a legal point of view, tries to make critical general statements regarding the effects of law on society. Such statements are usually devoid of legal meaning... Furthermore, the insider's understanding of the law is not simply a question of legal knowledge which might be acquired through formal legal education, but also a function of legal practice. In other words, one must also know how laws are used in practice, a tacit form of knowledge which can be acquired only through working within the legal system and gaining experience from legal practice. (Bannakar, 1997, p 9)

The 'disclosures' often attributed to sociologists include attempts to debunk the social status of law as a profession, to demystify the linguistic and symbolic trappings of legal proceedings, and to expose the ideological role of law in supporting the economic and social position of dominant groups in society (Bannakar, 1997, p 9). However, what jurists most resent about sociological accounts – and this also includes studies which describe language-use in the courtroom – is that they tell us very little about the content of legal practice.

Addressing different perspectives in the courtroom

The only way to gain access to the private world of courtrooms is to speak to practitioners, and attempt to understand the nature of their practical day-to-day tasks. I obtained access to the perspectives of adjudicators, representatives for the appellant, and representatives for the Home Office by obtaining permission to conduct ethnographic fieldwork inside three organisations. I spent 30 days, over a period of two months, studying the work of the Immigration Advisory Service, the largest organisation funded by the government that provides free advice and representation in the courts. I also spent 12 days over a 10-week period with adjudicators, and a few days in a unit of Presenting Officers working for the Home Office.

Obtaining access

Obtaining access turned out to be a lengthy business. Following the procedure described in standard texts on ethnography, I first wrote to 'gate-keepers', explaining my objectives, and enclosing copies of the grant applications I was making at the time, and then met a senior figure in the organisation, who put me in touch with managers, who then arranged access to practitioners.

Keith Best, the director of the Immigration Advisory Service (IAS), was immediately receptive to the idea of a project that would promote greater public understanding and awareness of immigration law, since this is also one of the official objectives of the IAS. The Immigration Appellate Authority has a good record of allowing academics to study the courts, but it took some time to arrange access through the Lord Chancellor's Department. I first wrote in the summer of 1994, and obtained permission to conduct the study in June 1996.

I had to send several letters to the Home Office before I made contact with the right department, but I was eventually given permission to observe the work of Presenting Officers in the unit that serves Thanet House. In each case, I promised to anonymise data, and to give the different organisations drafts of what I was planning to publish. I also sent regular reports about my progress and research questions.

Methods and objectives

The main research method I used was to follow practitioners around the courts, asking questions about the legal or evidential issues in particular appeals, whenever an opportunity arose during the working day. Recruits in all these organisations were expected to spend a few days 'shadowing' experienced practitioners, as part of their training, before being given their own cases or clients, so this was easy to arrange. There were even a few occasions when practitioners mistakenly assumed that I was a trainee, and passed on practical tips about different aspects of their day-to-day tasks.

Fieldwork with IAS counsellors

I began using this method to look at all aspects of work in the Hounslow and central London offices of the IAS, in order to get a feel for the different kinds of appeals being heard by the courts in Hatton Cross and Thanet House. I mostly accompanied counsellors to hearings before adjudicators, but I also attended some hearings at The Tribunal, the second tier of the appeals system, which was then based in Thanet House. For each appeal, I was usually able to read the file, and ask representatives about the legal and evidential issues involved.

About a month into this initial period of fieldwork, I made a strategic decision about the kind of data I would collect in the rest of the project. Instead of observing every aspect of legal work in the appeals system, I decided to concentrate on the work of practitioners in primary purpose and asylum appeals. This means that I will not be using this study to look at other cases involving family reunion (for example, concerning dependant relatives), students, businesses or deportations. I will have nothing to say about bail hearings (an important issue for anyone concerned with detentions). I will also be concentrating on work in the first tier of the system, although I will make some observations about The Tribunal in the next chapter.

Fieldwork with adjudicators

The method I used in studying the work of adjudicators was very similar, although I decided to limit myself to spending one day a week in the courts at Hatton Cross for the period between October and December 1996. I observed appeals from the public gallery, but had the opportunity to discuss the issues raised by the appeal before and after the hearing, and during any breaks. I also had lunch with the adjudicators, which gave an opportunity to hear them discuss legal and evidential issues, and exchange stories about their experience in particular hearings[6].

Understanding the technical content of immigration law

My main objective was to understand the technical content of immigration law, as this was used and applied in primary purpose and asylum appeals. Immigration is generally acknowledged to be a difficult and specialist area of legal work, due to the rapid growth in case-law, and the fact that it is necessary to understand a large and complex set of rules created by secondary as well as primary legislation. It should be remembered, however, that, in common with other areas of legal practice, most cases coming before the courts do not involve much law, because the rules and authorities governing many kinds of decision are already settled and agreed.

Chapters Four and Five of this study are, consequently, mostly about how adjudicators, and other practitioners, determined the facts in primary purpose and asylum appeals. They are not about 'hard cases', or how the law develops in the higher courts. However, this kind of routine interpretive work is important sociologically, since it determines the outcome of most appeals. I found that I was able to understand most aspects of the law relating to these cases, without any great difficulty, through reading the relevant law reports, and consulting legal handbooks[7].

Understanding the private world of the civil service

Despite some moves in the direction of 'open government', the British civil service is still very much a closed world, which is careful in dealing with outsiders[8]. Few ethnographers have obtained access to government bureaucracies in Britain (although, see Rock, 1994, 1995), and it is difficult obtaining documentary information (for example, minutes of meetings, or recommendations about policy to ministers) that are publicly available in some other political systems[9]. I did, however, conduct a small number of interviews with civil servants in the Lord Chancellor's Department and the Home Office, about their interest in immigration policy and the courts.

Many sociologists still tend to regard people with higher social status and incomes than themselves with considerable suspicion. One contribution to a recent text on methodological issues in "researching the powerful" (Walford, 1994) describes the world of civil servants as "another country" inhabited by people from different backgrounds, and talking a completely different language, to the sociologist:

> ... there is a class cultural dimension that is central to a full appreciation of policy research at this level.... It remains the case that, of the fast-track civil servants, that is, those selected for future advancement to high office, and who have frequent direct contact with ministers, about half still come from Oxbridge and independent school backgrounds.... We were not 'public school', nor had we been to Oxbridge. In interview situations, we encountered individuals who, by selection and training, had the capacity to present their department's case clearly and persuasively. They were at ease with the demands made of them to present well-developed accounts of a policy's features and its intentions. We joked to one another that these were respondents who set out their case not only in correct, connected English sentences, but in paragraphs as well. These cultural features were articulated with our respondents' abilities to work successfully within the conventions of civil service life. (Fitz and Halpin, 1994, p 42)

They also describe their difficulties in conducting research in "unfamiliar and intimidating" surroundings:

> It was the administrators' territory, a habitat with which they were familiar and in which they felt comfortable and confident. Thus the 'reality' that was narrated was inevitably highly constrained. We glimpsed an unfamiliar world that was only ever partially revealed. We were not privy, for example, to situations in which the political skills and reputations of ministers were discussed, [or] where civil service careers were forensically dissected. (Fitz and Halpin, 1994, p 40)

One cultural resource I was able to draw upon in studying civil servants was the fact I *had* been to Oxbridge, and I found little difficulty communicating with civil servants in these government departments. It was, however, hard obtaining specific information about the behind-the-scenes work involved in advising ministers, or steering legislation through Parliament. The civil servants I interviewed were open about the fact that there are many aspects to their work – for example, the range of policy options being considered by ministers – which *should* be concealed from the general public. However, they were willing to talk, in general terms, about their perspective on the courts, and the policy-making process. One interviewee described the objective of my project (to encourage debate and reflection about immigration control) as "essentially harmless".

The greatest problem I experienced in this part of the fieldwork was that, to begin with, I did not know enough about how government worked to ask the kind of questions that would produce detailed answers. Here is an extract from an interview about the making of the 1996 Asylum and Immigration Act which illustrates my initial ignorance about the work of civil servants:

MT: **Was there a feeling of pressure ... time pressure for people to get these things done, the various people working on the....**

C1: **Yes. I mean this was an important government priority that the government was keen to get into place as soon as was practicable. It was a high priority project.**

MT: **And it started in the autumn of last year, and it takes about a year to move from the initial....**

C2: **Well, the maximum period a Bill can take *is* a year [humorous moment at my display of ignorance] ... because of the parliamentary rule which says that a Bill has to be contained within a session. The government in this case created, I think, a slightly shorter time, a slightly shorter target time than it does for most of the legislation, and the rules were linked to some part of the Act which says there have to be some rules to make certain parts of the Act effective, so the timetables were tied.**

MT: **And you will internally have a timetable which links what you're going to do to that agenda. I suppose it's a bit like our course development....**

C2: **Yes, there is.... The Bill sort of drove it forward. The Rules timetable, which in the end proved to be a bit flexible, was tied to what was happening in the Bill, and I've got an administrative timetable to bring things into effect as a result of both the Act and the Rules.**

This demonstrates the kind of problem created by interviews, in which the interviewer has to discover what objects in the world, like a parliamentary Bill, mean as a practical matter to the people preparing legislation. It also shows how I could draw on my own experience of organisations, and the long timetable of meetings involved in changing course documents in higher education, to make sense of work in the civil service.

Understanding the private world of politicians

Politics is the most public of the worlds that concern me in this book. It is possible to follow debates and issues through watching television, reading the newspapers, attending public meetings, or from reading books and pamphlets produced by academics and pressure groups seeking to persuade society to adopt some change in public policy.

Britain's treatment of asylum-seekers was regularly in the news while I was conducting fieldwork in the courts, mainly because of the Conservative government's Asylum and Immigration Bill which was vigorously opposed by the Labour Party, but became law in September 1996. It has also been in the news during the enactment of the 1999 Immigration and Asylum Act. The immense volume of paper generated by the parliamentary process constitutes an important source of data for academics, who act as commentators and disseminators of information in the same process.

There is, however, good reason to be cautious about taking the public face of politics at face value. Although Chapter Seven goes some way in conveying the character of immigration as a political issue, I am conscious that there may well be a 'private world' that I have failed to address, through not getting close enough to the different groups who are concerned with making policy in political parties. I would expect, for example, that discussion inside particular political circles (for example, groups with strong views about immigration in the Labour and Conservative parties) has a different character to the discussion that takes place publicly in the media, and in parliament[10]. Government ministers, on the other hand, of whatever Party, often have to balance their own ideological preferences, with what is financially or 'politically' possible. How political life is understood by insiders has never been investigated, using ethnographic methods, by sociologists or political scientists (see Prus, 1997, p 147).

Understanding the world of the appellant

Most of this study looks at the courts from the point of view of legal practitioners, civil servants, campaigners or politicians. Perhaps the most interesting group for many readers will be the appellants: the people who are appealing against a government decision refusing them entry to the United Kingdom; or, in the case of asylum-seekers, turning down their request for refugee status.

For many sociologists, giving a voice to 'oppressed' groups, or 'victims' has almost taken on the character of a moral duty, but few studies have been successful in addressing how actual members of such groups understand their 'oppression' in day-to-day situations. This is partly because it is often hard obtaining access to people on the receiving end of government or judicial decisions, whether these are social security claimants, defendants in the criminal justice system, or asylum-seekers[11]. Many researchers have also tended to idealise group perspectives (for example, those of 'women' or 'blacks'), rather than investigating what might be a diverse range of experiences and viewpoints[12].

I have chosen not to include much discussion on the perspective of appellants in this book, although the transcripts in Chapters Four and Five illustrate how the sponsors in primary purpose appeals, and asylum-seekers, gave evidence in court. The whole determination process can be viewed, in some respects, as a series of opportunities for appellants to present their case to the government, and then to an independent adjudicator. However, there will also be a private dimension to the experience of appellants which is not available from attending hearings.

I also interviewed a small, and unrepresentative, number of asylum-seekers about their experiences, and was struck by their faith in the appeals process, despite the fact that some had been waiting years for a hearing, and by their determination to stay in Britain[13]. It seems unlikely that anyone who was really an economic migrant would reveal this to a sociologist. However, any serious interpretive study would have to find a way of addressing a wide range of experiences and perspectives. Asylum-seekers include people who have been tortured, and find it difficult talking to their own representatives. They also include people who have gone to immense lengths to enter the United Kingdom by fabricating an asylum claim, assisted by traffickers and other illegal organisations. From a sociological point of view, it would be interesting to learn more about the perspective of the 'bogus', as well as the 'genuine' asylum-seeker, by interviewing appellants.

Some missing perspectives

This chapter has been concerned with the methods I used to research these four social worlds, but it also seems important to acknowledge that there are many other perspectives I could have addressed in this study. During my fieldwork, I never looked at the role of solicitors or barristers in the courts in any detail, or at the agents who represent many appellants. I also never interviewed clerical and administrative staff in the courts (see Rock, 1993), or examined the perspective of editors and reporters in different newspapers.

There will be many overlapping social worlds in any complex institution like a court–system, and the researcher with limited time must inevitably have to make choices about which groups to interview, and in which organisations it is worth conducting fieldwork. There have, however, been few ethnographic studies about lawyers, judges, civil servants, or politicians, which examine these perspectives in any degree of depth. I hope that this preliminary attempt will encourage other researchers to use similar methods in investigating a range of groups concerned with immigration control.

Notes

[1] For an analysis of publicly-available data from the Kennedy Smith rape trial, see Matoesian (1997). The most recent trial in America which attracted widespread public interest was the case of Louise Woodward, a nanny who was charged with killing a child in her care.

[2] The business of these courts has since transferred to Taylor House, which is near the Sadler's Wells Theatre in Islington.

[3] The stature and authority of judicial officials can undoubtedly be enhanced by the architecture of courtrooms, and the designers of these hearing rooms may have tried to strike a balance between giving this support, but also making appellants and representatives feel comfortable. For discussion of how the spatial arrangements in courts can affect the conduct of hearings, see Carlen (1976), Atkinson and Drew (1979), and Rock (1993).

[4] The exception to this general lack of media interest in the courts was the appeal of the Islamic activist, Mohammed al-Masari, who had been sending subversive messages by fax to Saudi Arabia while he was claiming asylum in Britain. The

Home Secretary had offered him sanctuary on a British colony in the Caribbean, allegedly under economic pressure from the Saudi government. Dr al-Masari's appeal hearing at Wood Green, which resulted in the case being referred back to the Secretary of State, was widely reported in the quality press.

[5] In her (1981) study of the criminal justice system, Doreen McBarnet was also struck by the fact that almost no one visits magistrates' courts. For McBarnet, this is no accident: she argues that we are given the impression that justice is fair and impartial from the public spectacle that takes place in the higher courts, whereas the routine, repressive work of the State is protected by an "ideology of triviality".

[6] When the courts broke for lunch at 1.00 pm, the adjudicators were served sherry (a practice which is common in many of the higher courts), before eating around one large table. Paterson (1982), in his study of the Law Lords, also noted the importance of informal interaction in allowing judges to consult with colleagues. The importance of 'canteen culture' has also been noted in other occupations (for example, Holdaway, 1983).

[7] I could, of course, have learnt considerably more about immigration law, in the same period of time, by working as a representative or adjudicator, and learning the law through preparing submissions, or writing determinations for particular appeals. Becoming a complete participant was not, however, feasible in this research project, and would also have prevented me from taking notes during hearings.

[8] The civil service is now required to supply information about non-sensitive areas of policy on request, under an initiative introduced by John Major's Conservative government. More information is available to the public about the policy-making process, and the activities of different government agencies in countries like America, Canada and Australia. However, see the discussion about the reality of "freedom of information" in America in Calavita (1992, Chapter 1).

[9] Probably the best academic study about immigration control to date is Calavita's (1992) historical account of the development of American policy towards Mexican immigrants during the Braco program from 1942 to 1964 which draws upon interviews with ex-officials, and archives made available by the Immigration and Naturalization Service (INS). This is informed by an interest in how policies towards migrant labour were shaped by lobby groups within government, and divisions between different 'fractions' in the capitalist ruling class. For an

ethnographic study of the development of a policy initiative concerning victims of crime in a government ministry in Canada, see Rock (1986).

[10] I obtained some interesting glimpses into this world through attending public meetings organised by the campaign against the 1995 Asylum and Immigration Bill. It was, for example, apparent that there was a wide gulf on policy between left-wingers in the Labour Party, like Diane Abbott, and the front-bench leadership which never became public during the 1997 election campaign for 'political' reasons.

[11] There have been some notable exceptions, for example, Baldwin and McConville's (1977) study of plea-bargaining based on interviews with convicted defendants. Most studies about public sector organisations continue to be about the perspective of the managers and professionals who supply a service, rather than their clients.

[12] This is often accompanied by a claim to have a privileged insight into the experience of the oppressed group. Marxist theorists once used to make this claim about the 'working class'. Today, feminist standpoint theorists make exactly the same claim about the needs and experience of 'women' (see, for example, Smith, 1979), and similar arguments are employed by researchers claiming to speak on behalf of racial and ethnic minorities, or other groups such as homosexuals or disabled people.

[13] These interviews were arranged through the Refugee Legal Centre, and took place in the coffee bar at Hatton Cross, and an interview room in Lincoln House. They were unrepresentative in the sense that these were clients whom representatives liked, and believed (although this does not mean that they all obtained a successful outcome from the hearing).

THREE

The appeals process

The immigration courts are part of a larger administrative and judicial process that starts in the Home Office and is sometimes only concluded by an appeal to the House of Lords. This whole system has been subject to a great deal of criticism in recent years, and a number of changes will be made by the 1999 Immigration and Asylum Act. Some proposals have been quite radical: one consultation paper circulating in 1998 suggested that the whole second tier of the court-system could be abolished! Chapters Six and Seven examine how civil servants, politicians and pressure groups have understood the courts as an administrative problem. This chapter gives an overview of how the system worked while I was observing hearings in 1996. It summarises the main stages of decision making, and introduces the occupational groups working in the courts.

Four stages of decision making

Anyone seeking to enter the United Kingdom as an immigrant must apply for Entry Clearance from the British government. Similarly, anyone seeking asylum must apply for recognition as a Convention refugee. These decisions are made by civil servants working for the Home Office, but applicants have a right of appeal to the system of administrative tribunals, which I have been calling the British Immigration Courts.

There are four principal stages of decision making: the initial decision by the Home Office; a review by an adjudicator; a review by 'The Tribunal', the second tier of the immigration court-system; and a further review by the higher courts.

The Immigration and Nationality Department

Immigration control is the responsibility of the Immigration and Nationality Department (IND), a sub-division of the Home Office, based at Lunar House in Croydon. Decisions on marriage appeals, which I will be describing in the next chapter, are made by Entry Clearance Officers who work in British embassies and consulates abroad.

Unsuccessful applicants are sent a two- or three-page 'Explanatory Statement' setting out the reasons why they are being refused leave to enter Britain. Decisions on asylum applications are made by case-officers working in Croydon. Unsuccessful applicants receive a statement in the form of a 'letter of refusal' from the Secretary of State.

The immigration courts

Appeals to adjudicators

These are heard at centres in London, Hatton Cross, Manchester, Cardiff, Birmingham, Leeds and Glasgow. Appeals last an average of two hours (although, in some cases, it requires one or two days to hear the evidence). The format is similar to adversarial hearings in the civil or criminal courts in that witnesses are called, and then cross-examined by representatives acting for the appellant and the Home Office. There are then submissions from the representatives. Appellants are informed of the result of the appeal by a determination which is sent by post after the hearing[1].

The Tribunal

Unsuccessful appellants can appeal, with leave, to The Tribunal, a second tier of the court-system. Appeals are currently heard by a panel comprising two lay members and a legally-qualified chair who hear oral submissions from representatives[2]. They can be allowed or rejected, or remitted to the first tier for rehearing before a different adjudicator. No new evidence is presented in these hearings.

The higher courts

Any appellant who is refused leave to appeal to The Tribunal can apply to the High Court for judicial review of this decision. Appellants can also appeal to the Court of Appeal from The Tribunal[3].

An overview of the appeals process

The full process of administrative and judicial decision making in determining whether someone can be admitted as an immigrant, or as a Convention refugee, is represented in Figure 3.1.

Figure 3.1: The process of administrative and judicial decision making

Making an initial decision on an application
(Case-workers in Croydon/Entry Clearance Officers)

First tier of the immigration courts
(Legally qualified adjudicator sitting alone)

Second tier of the immigration courts
(The Tribunal: legally qualified chair and two lay-members)

Appeal to the Court of Appeal; or
application for Judicial Review by the High Court

Appeal to the House of Lords

Decisions made by civil servants in the Home Office, and by judges in the higher courts, can be important and consequential in deciding outcomes for both individuals and groups of appellants. This study will, however, only be concerned with the central part of the diagram, and especially the first tier of the immigration courts in which adjudicators hear appeals against decisions by the Home Office. The final decision on most claims for asylum is made at this stage of the decision-making process.

The legal framework of decison making

The key decisions about immigration and asylum in Britain are made by judges and other judicial officials, on a case-by-case basis. There are many texts by legal scholars which summarise and discuss this branch of English law (for example, MacDonald and Blake, 1995). From a sociological point of view, it is also interesting to consider the routine practices and assumptions which enable any court-system to operate. This section describes the doctrine of precedent at the heart of the English legal system, and the way in which information about previous decisions is circulated among practitioners.

The doctrine of precedent in English law

England has a system of law-making based on judges applying general principles derived from decisions made in previous cases to any new set of facts. This has been exported, through the British empire to America, Canada, Australia and the rest of 'the common law world'. The interpretive techniques employed by judges in making decisions constitute the discipline of black-letter law, which is taught to students in law schools.

The strength of this system, at least according to its admirers, is that it preserves continuity with the past, while giving judges considerable discretion in the way legal rules are applied to particular cases. In theory, at least, the facts of any case can be 'distinguished' from those in previous decisions, and so allow judges to develop the law, or make exceptions if they feel that this serves the interests of justice. It is also possible for judges to stop following precedents, when it is clear they have outlived their usefulness. Most cases involve applying established rules of law, and the main task of the courts is to decide the relevant facts.

The key principle underpinning the whole decision-making process is the doctrine of precedent or *stare decisis* (meaning 'to stand by what has been decided'). This requires judges to follow previous decisions. It also requires the lower courts to follow decisions made by the higher courts (the apex of the system being the House of Lords). Ultimately, however, the whole system is based upon the interpretive work of the judge in assessing previous cases.

A central assumption built into common law judicial systems is that judges can and will disagree about how to interpret the law. Decisions in the House of Lords are made by five Law Lords. Decisions in the Court of Appeal are usually made by three Lord Justices of Appeal. The majority view becomes the *ratio decidendi* (reason for the decision) in the case, and will bind all lower courts.

It has, however, been common for differences of opinion to emerge which have resulted in conflicting decisions about the same point of law. Lord Denning and Lord Donaldson were, for example, known for having strongly divergent views when they sat on the Court of Appeal. Many important areas of law were, therefore, left uncertain, in that judges in the lower courts could choose which precedents to follow until there was a binding decision by the House of Lords.

The development of immigration law

Immigration law comprises a set of statutes, statutory instruments, informal administrative policies and previously decided cases which are used by adjudicators in reaching decisions, and by representatives in advising their clients. The rules governing decision making in the immigration courts are similar to those in the rest of the legal system. Adjudicators will, in practice, be guided by decisions made by The Tribunal (although these are not, strictly speaking, binding), and are required to follow decisions by the Court of Appeal or House of Lords.

Owing to the relatively recent origins of this appeals system, there is still considerable uncertainty in many areas of immigration law. Some important principles, such as the definition of persecution in asylum appeals, remain uncertain, while others, such as the guidelines that should be followed in deciding the primary purpose of a marriage, were only established after four or five years of decisions in the higher courts. This is because the only way for a principle to be decided is for an appeal to be heard by the House of Lords. Moreover, the higher courts have been reluctant to rule on general principles that might have far-reaching consequences for government policy.

One informant summarised the slow development of precedents for asylum appeals in the following terms:

> "One of the big growth industries, if you like, in immigration, is asylum cases. There've always been asylum cases, but they have been few and far between, and cases have only occasionally gone up to the High Court. But because there are now such a huge volume of cases coming through, issues which previously had been, if you like, glossed over have come to the fore, and five years later the High Court are sitting deciding on points of law which, you know, it's quite remarkable they've never come to before. But the reason is because they've never seen such a volume of cases."

Interestingly, disputes about immigration law have developed in The Tribunal following a similar pattern to the disputes which have been common in the Court of Appeal. The two most senior members of The Tribunal, while I was doing my fieldwork, had been working in the courts since the mid–1980s, and it was well known that they took different approaches in deciding appeals. Professor Jackson adopted a 'literal', or narrow approach towards interpreting the immigration rules, which often resulted in a decision that favoured the appellant. Mr Madison employed a more 'robust' or critical approach in considering what the legislators meant to achieve by the rule, which often resulted in the Home Office winning the appeal.

The outcome of many appeals was determined by which chair happened to be sitting that day, and this was recognised by representatives. As one Presenting Officer put it:

> **"There is still the situation where if you know who your ... tribunal chair is, then you prepare your case accordingly.... Perhaps you understand the chair's views on particular types of cases because you may remember the precedent of a similar case which he or she has dealt with, and you can go in on that basis.... I think that most accept that they don't have the same approach to immigration law."**

The circulation of precedents

In order for judges to be bound by precedents, they need to keep up-to-date with previously-decided cases. The most important of these are published as law reports: important decisions about immigration law are published in a series known as the Green Books, which are edited by a member of The Tribunal.

It is not, however, only reported cases that influence adjudicators and tribunals in deciding new appeals. Other decisions are also circulated among adjudicators and representatives, along with regular digests summarising developments that are taking place in the law. For practical reasons, not every practitioner can read all the thousands of decisions made on any one day throughout the court-system. However, every single decision is sent to research officers, working in the main organisations, or professional associations serving the courts, who identify possible precedents, and summarise these for practitioners. Adjudicators can ask the research officer employed by the Immigration Appellate Authority for advice on any point of law in the course of writing their determinations.

The legal character of the appeals system

The appeals process can, in this sense, be viewed as a system for producing law, as much as outcomes for appellants. However, it should also be recognised that much of the routine business of the courts requires very little discussion of legal rules. Even day-to-day work in The Tribunal, which, one might imagine, involves more discussion of legal arguments, is mostly administrative in character. A great deal of time is spent hearing complaints that adjudicators have not followed the correct procedures in hearing evidence or writing up their determinations.

There are, however, hearings which do involve a dispute over a point of law. On one visit to The Tribunal, I observed the case of an American citizen who had applied to enter Britain as the sole representative of a business which was concerned with the distribution of 'girlie' magazines. He had been refused leave to enter, after having already obtained a visa, for making a false representation in the application form. The appeal turned on the construction of the word 'material' in the relevant section of the immigration rules, since the false representation was made in a section of the form that was not relevant ('material') to his application for a particular type of 'entry status'.

The chair of The Tribunal surprised both representatives by raising a legal point about 'materiality' that had been left undecided in a previous majority judgment by the Court of Appeal. He adjourned the appeal for four months so that each side could read this case and present legal arguments. However, it was clear to everyone that the ultimate objective was to send the case up to the Court of Appeal. One representative summarised the hearing in the following terms:

> **"I was trying to establish at the beginning what my parameters were, and he then jumped to the evidence … and I could only respond to his questions. He had his own agenda. I mean, he always does have his own agenda. But then this is the sort of case he likes to get his teeth into. There's a nice meaty legal argument that he's created for himself."**

This illustrates how it was possible for a tribunal chair to raise a point of law, even though this had not been included in the grounds for appeal submitted by the appellant. His decision at the next hearing could then be appealed by either of the parties. An eventual judgment by the Court of Appeal, provided it was made by a majority of judges, would be binding on The Tribunal and adjudicators, unless the facts could be distinguished from those in this case.

The courtroom community

Courtrooms can also be understood as occupational communities, in which practitioners meet regularly in hearings, and coordinate their activities to process large numbers of cases (Blumberg, 1969; Emerson, 1969; Feeley, 1979; Rock, 1993). This section introduces the main occupational groups working in the immigration courts[4].

Adjudicators

The central task of adjudicators is to decide the outcome of appeals through applying the relevant law to the evidence presented in hearings. Most of their time is spent in court, where they are expected to get through a list of between two and three appeals in each working day. They also have to review the evidence, and write up determinations, outside hearings[5].

Becoming an adjudicator

The Immigration Appellate Authority employs about 250 adjudicators, most of whom sit an average of between one and two days per week. The salary for a full-time adjudicator in 1996 was £68,000 per annum. They are required to be over the age of 35, and to have at least four years post-qualification experience as a barrister or solicitor. The majority are men nearing or past retirement age, but there are also a fair number of younger men and women, and people from different ethnic backgrounds.

Adjudicators come to work in the courts for a variety of reasons, which will be apparent from the following cases:

Adjudicator 1: He had originally qualified as a barrister, but had spent most of his career working as a diplomat for the Foreign Office, based mainly in East and West Africa, but also in the Far East. He had retired early for personal reasons, and was doing this as a 'semi-retirement job'. He sat two days a week.

Adjudicator 2: He had retired after a career as a solicitor in a commercial law firm, and had approached the Lord Chancellor's Department, looking for a judicial job of some kind. He had been given the opportunity to do immigration, and was told that in one year he could apply for jobs in other tribunals. He also ran a computer company, and was a director of a small London theatre. He sat two days per week.

Adjudicator 3: He was a solicitor, specialising in immigration cases. His firm had already started to attract more business, since word quickly got around the local Asian community that he was now an adjudicator. He sat one day a week.

Adjudicator 4: He was a solicitor, working in a medium-sized general practice. He had wanted 'to do something a bit different' at this stage of his career, which would involve working shorter hours, and with less stress than fee-paying work. He had arranged with his firm to take a drop in income, so that he could sit two days per week.

Adjudicator 5: She was a young woman, from a West African background, who had qualified as a barrister, and now did part-time work lecturing at the College of Law, as well as sitting on this, and two other tribunals.

Becoming a part-time adjudicator can, therefore, be something to do in retirement (Adjudicators 1 and 2), a means of promoting your firm to immigration clients (Adjudicator 3), a life-style choice (Adjudicator 4), or a career, combined with other part-time work, in its own right (Adjudicator 5).

Training

Adjudicators are required to attend a three-day residential course for immigration appeals, and those who are appointed as 'special adjudicators' (meaning that they can hear asylum appeals) take a further two-day course. These courses introduce the relevant law and procedures regulating the courts through lectures, exercises about legal and procedural problems, a mock appeals hearing, and a workshop on determination writing. They are also required to spend five days sitting with an experienced adjudicator, before hearing their own appeals[6].

Making decisions

The task of assessing evidence in the immigration courts does not require specialist training or knowledge. The adjudicator is, in this sense, exactly like a member of a jury who has to reach a decision about the facts of a case, through hearing witnesses, and reading documentary evidence. Adjudicators recognise that there are no objective criteria they can use in assessing evidence, other than their own intuition and judgment. As one observed:

> **"You've got the law and your instinct in dealing with these cases, and have to be able to size up people. And two adjudicators might differ, like in a jury."**

To this extent, any reader of this book is equally well placed to assess the evidence presented to adjudicators in appeals hearings. Any reader would also experience the same difficulty in making decisions about particular appellants. One adjudicator described these in the following terms:

> **"[In political asylum appeals] it can be a life or death decision. You can sometimes agonise, and it can keep me up at night. I had an Iranian case. I had a lot of sympathy. This lad had suffered a terrible depression, and was no harm to anybody. They're mainly people in the mountains, and in a bad way mentally, and he couldn't continue with his evidence after giving evidence-in-chief. I eventually couldn't.... At first, I thought it was one I can allow, but I couldn't. But I could make a recommendation. Then at least I feel I've done what is right. Even if the Secretary of State doesn't follow me, at least I'm not responsible for his actions."**

Making a 'recommendation' involves finding against the appellant, but requesting that the Home Office exercise its discretion outside the immigration rules by granting Exceptional Leave to Remain. Adjudicators also know that, if they do make a mistake, the appellant has a good chance of being given leave to appeal to The Tribunal.

———

Managing hearings

The adjudicator's main task in the hearing is to make a summary of the evidence. In addition, they have to manage witnesses, interpreters, and representatives, and respond to any procedural problems, such as requests for an adjournment.

Some adjudicators intervene very little during hearings. Others, however, adopt an inquisitorial role in questioning witnesses while they give evidence. They also sometimes interrupt closing submissions to establish the key points that a representative should be addressing, or to prevent them from developing certain lines of argument[7].

To manage hearings smoothly, and with an air of authority or competence, requires some degree of preparation before the hearing. One adjudicator I sat with made a chronology of the history of the file, so he could see at a glance what had occurred, if a procedural question was raised. Another taught me how to use an *aide memoire* during hearings where there were a number of witnesses: she made a list of their names, and, as they were introduced, made a note of some distinguishing feature which would enable her to identify them later in the hearing (for example, 'Mrs V – yellow sari'). This technique is also used in other occupations, which require practitioners to remember large numbers of names as part of their day-to-day work.

Presenting Officers

Home Office Presenting Officers (or 'HOPOs' as they are called in the courts) have an equivalent role to prosecutors in the criminal courts. The majority are civil servants, who are not legally qualified.

Becoming a Presenting Officer

Some Presenting Officers have been working in the courts for 20 years, and have much in common with legal executives in law firms who often specialise, and become expert in particular areas of law, without being solicitors or barristers. Others expect to work in this part of the civil service for only a few years, before moving to a completely different post[8].

While I was doing my fieldwork, a further group joined the Home Office on three-year contracts, who were not expected to stay in the civil service. Most had completed the academic stage of legal training, but were unable to find a pupillage or training contract in the legal profession, owing to the continuing effects of the economic recession of the early 1990s. They saw the immigration courts as an opportunity to gain experience as advocates, rather than as a long-term career.

The experience of one interviewee illustrates how it is possible to join the civil service as a graduate, and end up working in the immigration courts. She had become a civil servant in 1991, and had held a number of different posts, before becoming a Presenting Officer. She described her career in the following terms:

> **"I actually hoped to join the Foreign Office. I got to the final interview, and went through all the various stages, but they said you're close, but it's probably not appropriate for you at this time.... A letter came through saying we've contacted the Home Office and they can give you the position of an Entry Clearance Officer in a post overseas, and transfer over that way, which is what I did. I went out to Delhi and was a visa officer, and I put a feeler out to transfer to the Foreign Office, but I'd done a few years with the Home Office by then, so the incentive had really gone."**

When she returned to England, she worked in the public enquiries room at Lunar House for four-and-a-half-years. She was then given the opportunity to work for a temporary period as a Presenting Officer to gain work experience, and anticipated moving to a completely different job in the Home Office in a year's time.

The work of Presenting Officers

Presenting Officers have a role similar to barristers working for the Crown Prosecution Service in that they receive files prepared by civil servants in different parts of the Home Office, usually a week before the hearing. They have to be prepared to present six cases each day, although most of these will be adjourned. In contrast to the Crown Prosecution Service, they have no discretion over how to conduct appeals. One interviewee suggested that it was sometimes possible to withdraw 'weak' cases, depending on the attitude of case-workers:

> **"We are the barristers, and they are the people instructing us, and in very simple terms you could say that it's the Presenting**

Officer's job to present whatever they're given, regardless of whether they think it's meritorious or not.... Now that is where you start from. I personally think that that's ridiculous ... I think that Presenting Officers have got a considerable amount of experience of what will wash and won't wash, you know, in a pseudo Court of Law.... So the Presenting Officer ... will make contact with the case-worker in advance if they have issues to clear up, and they will seek to convince them that such and such needs to be changed about the paper work they've been provided with...."

From the back of the courtroom, there often appear to be big differences in the way Presenting Officers approach their work. Some cross-examinations have the character of the kind of exchanges one can observe in other courts: they take the form of a series of linked questions, directed at weaknesses or contradictions in the account given to the court during an examination-in-chief, with the aim of suggesting that the witness is lying. Most, however, have a perfunctory quality to them, which may reflect the limited time to prepare appeals, or the fact that Presenting Officers usually have no prior experience as advocates. Some cross-examinations are extremely short; and others more or less repeat the questions asked by the representative for the appellant.

The Immigration Advisory Service

About 50% of appellants are represented by two organisations which are funded by the Home Office. The largest of these, the Immigration Advisory Service (IAS), was established in the 1970s as the United Kingdom Immigration Advisory Service (UKIAS), and represents appellants in both immigration and asylum appeals. It has offices in London, Hounslow, Manchester, Birmingham, Cardiff and Glasgow, and employs a mixture of part-time and full-time staff, from a wide range of ethnic groups. A second organisation serving the courts is the Refugee Legal Centre, which is based in London.

Many people working in the IAS have no legal qualifications. However, it has taken on increasing numbers of staff who have completed the academic stage of legal training but have been unable to find jobs in the legal profession.

Advising and representing appellants has much in common with other types of 'contentious' legal work (see, for example, Mann, 1985; Travers,

1997b). It involves such tasks as researching the relevant law, taking instructions, giving advice, and presenting a case in court.

Clients in the IAS are initially seen by an advice worker, and then referred to a counsellor, who will represent them at the appeal. In many cases, counsellors have to meet clients on a few occasions before they feel sufficiently confident to make a statement. Clients are also asked to supply any documents that might help their case. In asylum appeals, these might be letters corroborating the appellant's evidence, or newspaper reports about recent political events.

Preparing for a case also involves researching the law, through obtaining copies of any relevant cases which can be presented to the adjudicator. In asylum cases, it involves compiling a dossier about the current situation in the appellant's country of origin.

In the hearings I observed, many counsellors adopted the tactic of putting any difficult questions to the witness during the examination-in-chief, so that this often took the form of a gentle cross-examination[9]. This makes it more difficult for the Presenting Officer to adopt an aggressive stance towards the witness, and may partly explain the relatively short length of some cross-examinations.

The counsellors I met were convinced that the most important single factor influencing the outcome of an appeal was the adjudicator. They knew, from experience, that most adjudicators would dismiss most appeals, although there were one or two 'liberals' who usually took a different view of the evidence[10]. They also recognised a distinction between adjudicators who were 'straight-down-the-line', or 'tough but fair', and those who dismissed every appeal.

It was, however, impossible for counsellors to predict with complete certainty the outcome of *any* appeal, notwithstanding their previous experience with particular adjudicators, or their own assessment of the case. A lot depended upon how witnesses came across during the hearing, and even then what appeared to be a hopeless case could still be allowed by the 'hardest' of adjudicators. For some of the representatives I met, these surprise results kept up their morale in representing appellants.

Insiders and outsiders

All the groups I have described knew each other well, and had a good working relationship. Some firms of solicitors, and barristers specialising in immigration law, were also viewed as insiders in this court-system. There were also, however, other practitioners who were viewed as outsiders, because they created problems for the day-to-day disposal of appeals.

Many complaints were made about small firms of solicitors in the legal aid sector of the profession. The problem here was that legal aid was only available for giving advice under the Green Form Scheme, and did not cover representation at hearings (Smith, 1992)[11]. Court insiders complained that appellants were often 'strung along' by unscrupulous solicitors, and abandoned on the day of the hearing.

Another group making a living from the courts were commercial agents. They offered a service to immigrants and asylum-seekers who distrusted government agencies, and preferred dealing with members of their own ethnic group. Their offices were often located on high streets in areas where there were high concentrations of immigrants, and sought to attract clients who might otherwise have gone to the IAS or charitable organisations[12].

Commercial agents were regarded with considerable suspicion and distaste by the rest of the courtroom community. A common complaint was that they charged high fees, without offering a proper service[13]. A leaflet circulated by one firm in London offered to obtain visas and entry clearance for clients among its other services, which gave the impression that it was possible to gain entry to the United Kingdom through paying the Home Office.

Many hope that the 1999 Immigration and Asylum Act will curb the activities of agents, through establishing a compulsory registration scheme. There are, however, no plans to require solicitors to join this scheme, or to extend legal aid to cover representation at hearings.

Notes

[1] In some of the appeals I observed, the adjudicator gave a decision immediately. These were usually cases where a decision was made in favour of the appellant.

[2] The 1999 Immigration and Asylum Act will make some important changes to The Tribunal, unless these sections are removed or amended in the committee stage of the legislative process. In future, appeals will be heard by paper submissions, rather than in oral hearings, with the aim of speeding up the decision-making process. It will also remove the requirement to have two lay-members on the panel to assist the legally-qualified chair.

[3] Section 9 of the 1988 Immigration Act introduced a direct right of appeal from The Tribunal to the Court of Appeal, in an attempt to restrict the use of applications

to the High Court for Judicial Review. It usually takes a few months for the Court of Appeal to hear an appeal, whereas it takes about a year for the High Court to decide an application for Judicial Review.

[4] See also Juss (1993, Chapter 5).

[5] This glosses a great deal of routine work. Determinations had to be typed, and checked, often more than once, before they were sent out to appellants. Owing to a shortage of administrative staff, this could take several weeks.

[6] Adjudicators told me that it took about a year to feel competent in hearings, given that the job involved learning about all kinds of administrative procedures as well as hearing evidence. Representatives would usually assist if they were unsure about a point of law or procedure, but it was sometimes necessary to have a short adjournment to consult with more experienced colleagues.

[7] Some adjudicators felt that it was necessary to interrupt representatives to save the time of the court, or to give the appellant a fair hearing if a representative was not asking relevant questions. Representatives tended to characterise this as 'rudeness', or to complain that particular adjudicators were unfair to appellants in the way they conducted the hearing.

[8] According to one informant, there was a period when becoming a Presenting Officer was the only way to get promoted up the salary scale in the Home Office. This is because not many civil servants wanted a post which required speaking in court.

[9] Some counsellors read from a list of prepared questions in the hearing. Others used a checklist of issues, and thought up the wording of questions on the spot.

[10] This illustrates the care that must be taken in assessing interview accounts, since according to their annual reports, the IAS and Refugee Legal Centre are successful in about 20% of their appeals.

[11] Immigration is an area of legal practice which has expanded as solicitors have lost monopolies in other areas of work, such as conveyancing.

[12] Another type of agent connected with the courts were members of different ethnic communities who arranged representation for clients, and offered their

services as translators during the interview. I was told that some agents would say anything to persuade the appellant to part with a higher fee.

[13] Similar accounts exist about the experience of Jewish immigrants in Britain in the late 19th century at the hands of agents from their own communities. See, for example, Gartner (1960).

FOUR

The primary purpose rule
and the courts

My aim in this chapter is to examine the work involved in representing appellants, and deciding appeals concerned with the primary purpose rule, which became part of British immigration law in the early 1980s, and was abolished by the Labour government that won power in May 1997. Even when it existed, some legal textbooks described this rule as a "sordid episode in immigration history" (Bevan, 1986), or as "this cruel rule" (Sachdeva, 1993), and expressed the hope that it would quickly be repealed. Now this has actually happened, this chapter is of only historical interest, although I can perhaps provide a more dispassionate account of the legal work involved in deciding particular appeals than would have been possible when the rule was a live political issue in the 1980s.

I begin the chapter by providing a short history of the rule, and then describe some aspects of the legal and evidential issues in six appeals, drawing upon my record of the hearings, and the determinations. I then discuss some factors taken into account by adjudicators in their decision making, drawing upon these case studies.

The history of the rule

The primary purpose rule can be understood as a successful attempt by successive governments to restrict or delay secondary immigration to the United Kingdom through marriage, following the end of most primary immigration after the 1962 Commonwealth Immigrants Act. It has particularly affected, and been directed against, further immigration from Asia, although white men have also experienced problems in marrying women from Third World countries such as the Philippines.

A detailed history of the rule can be found in Sachdeva (1993), which is especially useful in explaining how restrictions on immigration through marriage were revised, or in his words, "fine-tuned", a number of times during the 1970s and 1980s in response to changing political pressures and circumstances (see also Dummett and Nicol, 1990). I will now provide a short summary of this history to provide some context to how the rule was being used in the last year of its existence in 1996.

Restrictions on marriage in the 1960s

There were no attempts to restrict immigration through marriage while Britain was still admitting primary immigrants during the 1960s. However, after 1968 commentators began to suggest that men from the Indian subcontinent, who were refused entry under the Commonwealth Immigration Act, were using marriage as a means of circumventing immigration controls. The system of entry clearance, which was set up in 1968, and then formalised in 1969, was directed mainly against this type of secondary immigration, and Entry Clearance Officers were directed to impose strict limits on husbands and fiancés.

The restoration of sexual equality in 1974

There was a sustained campaign against this policy during the early 1970s by MPs acting on behalf of constituents affected by the rule, many of whom were white women who wanted to bring over a partner from outside the European Economic Community. This culminated in the introduction of a Private Member's Bill, the Spouses of UK Citizens (Equal Treatment) Bill of 1974. However, the Bill was withdrawn when the Labour government responded to pressure and changed the rules.

The refusal of 'marriages of convenience' after 1977

The immediate result of the 1974 rule change was an increase in the number of men seeking entry to the United Kingdom through marriage. In response, the government gave immigration officers powers under the 1977 Rules to refuse entry to those suspected of entering into a 'marriage of convenience'. This led to large numbers of men being refused entry to Britain in the late 1970s. However, because many were genuine marriages, this only had a limited effect in restricting secondary immigration through marriage from the subcontinent.

The introduction of the primary purpose rule in 1980

The Conservative government that was elected in 1979 was committed to a much tougher policy in restricting secondary immigration from

---

Asia. To begin with, it wished to restore the controls removed by Labour in 1974, which had prevented all husbands and fiancés from entering the country. At the same time, however, it devised a means of protecting the position of white women, who had been one of the main political factors behind the rule change in 1974. The rules issued in 1980 did this by preventing husbands or fiancés obtaining entry clearance for settlement, *unless* they were joining British citizens who had been born in the United Kingdom. They also established the requirement, for the first time, that entry clearance would be refused if an Entry Clearance Officer had reason to believe that the 'primary purpose' of the marriage was 'to obtain admission to the United Kingdom'.

The 1983 rules

According to Sachdeva (1993, pp 84-8) and MacDonald (1987), this clause about the 'primary purpose' of a marriage was little used in the period 1980-83, because male applicants could be refused simply on the grounds that they were not joining British citizens who had been born in the United Kingdom. By 1983, however, the issue of primary purpose had become central to British immigration control since the government was forced to liberalise the rules to pre-empt a ruling by the European Court of Human Rights[1]. The new rules again allowed *all* female British citizens to be joined by their fiancés or husbands.

However, the 1983 rules were also made considerably tougher, as a concession to the anti-immigration wing of the Conservative party, by placing the burden of proof on the applicant. It was now up to the applicant to show that the 'primary purpose' of the marriage was not 'to enter the United Kingdom'. Many proved unable to do this, at least to the satisfaction of Entry Clearance Officers, when they were interviewed about their reasons for entering into the marriage.

Other restrictions on secondary immigration through marriage

British governments have always responded to political pressures to liberalise immigration control since the 1970s by making some concessions, while at the same time introducing further restrictions to placate political groups in favour of tougher controls. In 1977, the move back to sexual equality was accompanied by the introduction of a 'probationary period' so that the immigration service could investigate whether, in fact, a couple were living together in a genuine marriage. The probationary period has always been a year, although there was a proposal in 1983, when the government changed the rules under pressure from the European Court, to extend this to two years.

One new restriction that was introduced in 1984 was a much tougher requirement on applicants to show that they had adequate accommodation, and would be able to live in the United Kingdom without having recourse to state benefits. 'Maintenance and accommodation' has become a ground for refusing a substantial numbers of applicants, alongside primary purpose.

The final version of the rule

The main elements of the rule which governed entry of fiancés and spouses to Britain while I was doing my fieldwork had been established in 1984, although the most recent version had been issued by the Home Office in 1994 (HC395). The main provisions are worth presenting in full:

> **Fiancés (paragraph 47): A passenger seeking to enter the United Kingdom for marriage to a person present and settled in the United Kingdom or who is on the same occasion being admitted for settlement, and who intends to settle thereafter must hold a current entry clearance granted for that purpose. An entry clearance will be refused unless the entry clearance officer is satisfied:**
>
> (a) **that it is not the primary purpose of the intended marriage to obtain admission to the United Kingdom; and**
>
> (b) **that there is an intention that the parties to the marriage should live together permanently as man and wife; and**
>
> (c) **that the parties to the proposed marriage have met; and**
>
> (d) **that adequate maintenance and accommodation without recourse to public funds will be available for the applicant until the date of the marriage; and**
>
> (e) (i) **that there will thereafter be separate accommodation for the parties and their dependants without recourse to public funds in accommodation of their own or which they occupy themselves; and**

(ii) that the parties will thereafter be able to maintain themselves and their dependants adequately without recourse to public funds.

Spouses (paragraph 50): A passenger seeking admission to the United Kingdom as the spouse of a person who is present and settled in the United Kingdom, or who is on the same occasion being admitted for settlement, must hold a current entry clearance granted for that purpose. An entry clearance will be refused unless the entry clearance officer is satisfied:

(a) that the marriage was not entered into primarily to obtain admission to the United Kingdom; and

(b) that each of the parties has the intention of living permanently with the other as his or her spouse; and

(c) that the parties to the marriage have met; and

(d) that there will be adequate accommodation for the parties and their dependants without recourse to public funds in accommodation of their own or which they occupy themselves; and

(e) that the parties will be able to maintain themselves and their dependants adequately without recourse to public funds.

This test was used by Entry Clearance Officers, and adjudicators in determining whether someone was entitled to settle in the United Kingdom through marriage from 1984 to 1996.

The development of case-law on the primary purpose rule

By the time I did my fieldwork, the law on primary purpose was already settled. The same leading cases were cited by most advocates in their submissions, and followed by adjudicators in deciding the outcome of particular appeals. However, it is important to remember that the law only took on this settled character after a great deal of interpretive work by decision makers at different levels of the appeals system during the 1980s.

Legal writers usually present the development of immigration law as a series of landmark cases, as decision makers are faced with the practical problem of how to interpret particular rules and apply them to different factual situations (for example, Bevan, 1986). After a period of uncertainty, a principle will develop that judges or decision makers will follow, although later judgments might 'refine' or 'erode' the principle, or even revise it completely. For most of the time, adjudicators will apply the same rule or test in deciding appeals. But there were also times during the 1980s, when the law was unclear or uncertain; and appellants, the Home Office and adjudicators were waiting for an authoritative decision of the higher courts to establish some basic principles in interpreting the immigration rules.

It is difficult, after the event, to reconstruct how issues of law were understood by practitioners in the early years of the primary purpose rule. According to Sachdeva (1993, Chapter 4), the main issue for the courts was how to interpret the weight that should be given to different subsections of the rule. He identifies four main stages in the case-law.

Early decisions (1984–85)

There were a series of early tribunal decisions which suggested that, provided an adjudicator was satisfied about the genuineness of the marriage (subsection (b) of the rule), then the burden of proof was placed on the Home Office to establish that the primary purpose was to enter the United Kingdom. This was a view of the law which favoured the appellant.

Bhatia (1985)

This was a tribunal decision against the run of these cases which was eventually supported by the Court of Appeal. It returned the burden of proof to the appellant. There were also some comments when it went for Judicial Review, and in the Court of Appeal, which suggested that Entry Clearance Officers should be suspicious about the motives behind most arranged marriages. The judgment, therefore, resulted in more applications being refused, and in more appeals being dismissed by adjudicators.

Kumar (1986)

This judgment of the Court of Appeal did not change the burden of proof, but it did make it considerably easier for appellants to succeed in marriage cases. This is because adjudicators were asked to place greater weight on what had happened after the marriage in deciding appeals. If a couple could demonstrate 'intervening devotion', or there had been a child from the marriage, this would 'throw a flood of light' on the issue of primary purpose. This was an important decision in that the adjudicator who refused Kumar had stated that "under the rules, a marriage primarily entered into in order to obtain admission into the United Kingdom would still retain its non-qualifying character whatever happened afterwards, and even if the husband applied for entry on their Golden Wedding day". Now, anyone who married, and could demonstrate 'intervening devotion', had a good chance of satisfying the primary purpose rule.

Hoque and Singh (1988)

This was an important case in the sense of confirming the principles established by previous cases (and it contained a set of guidelines for adjudicators). It followed *Bhatia* on the issue of burden of proof, while advising decision makers to keep an open mind about the purpose of arranged marriages. It also supported *Kumar*, although it allowed Entry Clearance Officers to retain the discretion to refuse applicants, because of suspicion of their motives in entering into the marriage, even when there was evidence of 'intervening devotion'.

Cases after *Hoque and Singh*

There was no major change to the law following *Hoque and Singh*, although appeals continued to be made to The Tribunal and the Court of Appeal. Some decisions, like *Safter*, were extremely favourable to the appellant; others like *Sumeina Masood* (heard by Lord Justice Glidewell, the judge who later chaired the Glidewell Panel during the passage of the 1996 Asylum and Immigration Act) went further than previous cases in questioning the genuineness of arranged marriages. There were also a spectrum of decisions in between, and adjudicators had some discretion in how they interpreted *Hoque and Singh*[2].

The end of the rule

According to Sachdeva, refusals of applications for husbands and fiancés rose dramatically in the first year of the rule, and remained high into the 1990s, although it appears that official statistics were not kept after 1988. There was, however, a major change of policy in 1992, when the Home Office announced that it would no longer contest appeals where it could be demonstrated that a marriage had lasted five years, or where there had been a child. Sachdeva suggests that this was done because of a judgment by the European Court of Justice which made it possible for couples who were already in the United Kingdom to circumvent the rule by temporarily moving to Europe[3]. Another reason might be that, following *Kumar*, more and more appeals were being allowed, probably because most applications for entry were being made by husbands and wives rather than fiancés.

The Labour Party announced that it intended to abolish the rule during the election campaign of April 1997. Shortly after the election, the Home Office announced that all outstanding appeals would be temporarily taken out of the list, while the policy was reviewed by the new government. In June, it was announced that the rule itself was to be abolished, and the Home Office issued a statutory instrument which amended the HC395 immigration rules. The new rules contained the same text in paragraphs 47 and 50, although without the two lines in subsection (a) of each paragraph which established the rule.

The primary purpose rule in action

In the next part of this chapter, I will summarise the legal and evidential issues in six appeals I observed in the courts. I will be drawing upon the notes I made during each hearing, and copies of the determinations. I will also be drawing upon informal interviews with practitioners about the general issues raised by primary purpose cases, but also about the specific issues raised by these appeals. In three of the appeals, I was 'shadowing' a counsellor from the Immigration Advisory Service (IAS), and in the remaining three appeals I was 'shadowing' an adjudicator. The main witness in these appeals was the 'sponsor', the United Kingdom citizen whom the appellant had either married, or was intending to marry. The appellants were not present, since they had been refused permission to enter the United Kingdom.

Appeal I

This was the appeal of Miss C, a 28-year-old Filipino woman, that was heard in March 1996. She had applied to enter the United Kingdom as the fiancée of Mr R, a 59-year-old British man in November 1994.

Miss C had once been a member of a pen-pal club which arranged introductions between Filipino women and foreign men. She had also given her photograph to a friend who was visiting the United Kingdom. Mr R saw the photograph, and wrote to her in June 1991. They had then developed a relationship through corresponding, and Mr R had proposed in November 1992. They first met in 1994, when Mr R visited for a month. There were no disputed facts in the case, other than Miss C's reasons for accepting the proposal.

The Entry Clearance Officer gave a number of reasons for refusing the application on the grounds of primary purpose. One was the 30-year age gap, and the fact that the two 'would appear to have nothing in common'. Another was that Miss C had once been a member of a pen-pal club, and had been in correspondence with a Dutch man. A third was that she came from a poor economic background.

When I spoke to the counsellor the day before this appeal, she was optimistic about the result:

> **"We have good evidence of intervening devotion between the appellant and the sponsor.... Our sponsor will make a very good witness, and it appears that the applicant is quite genuine as well.... You'll meet the sponsor tomorrow – he's not a gullible sponsor, this one."**

The evidence of 'intervening devotion' was the long letters exchanged between the couple, which allowed her to show how the relationship developed.

In the hearing, the adjudicator also seemed to concentrate on establishing if this was a 'gullible sponsor'. The following is an example of the kind of exchange that took place in the hearing:

> A: **Well, what we're really concerned with is why it was she wanted to correspond and ultimately to move here. The question that concerns us is whether she was really doing this to get entry to the country, or to form a stable relationship. What I'd ask you to help with is why it was.**

> Was she primarily looking to get into this country? Or was she really looking for a husband?

W: I don't think she was looking. I think the love moved between us, and it's this love that now makes us want to be together.

A: Alright. If you thought what she was really doing was looking for someone to give her a passport into this country, would you go along with it?

W: No, Sir. May I clarify. The reason I would not want to go along is because I'd feel the love we feel would not be true, Sir, and consequently we could never be happy.

A: Do you feel her feelings are true?

W: Yes, Sir.

A: And what's the basis? I know it's terribly difficult, but why do you say that?

According to the counsellor, a deciding factor in the appeal might have been that Mr R had been in the armed forces. In the determination, the adjudicator accepted his assessment of Miss C's motives in becoming engaged:

> "I attach substantial weight to Mr R's opinion that Miss C's feelings for him are genuine. Having seen him, I believe he is well able to determine, and would have recognised any falsity. He is a man who has been about in the world. He knows the ways of men and women."

Unusually, the adjudicator gave the result of the appeal to the parties at the end of the hearing. After the submissions, he simply said:

> "Yes, thank you. I will allow the appeal, but I will reserve my determination and give you my reasons in writing to allow the appeal."

Appeal 2

This was an appeal by Mr M, a Bangladeshi man who was seeking to join his wife in the United Kingdom, following an arranged marriage that had taken place in December 1994. It was heard in December 1997. The wife was referred to in the hearing as Miss D.

This was a traditional arranged marriage between first cousins, who were members of an extended family which shared the same compound in their home village in Bangladesh. Miss D worked for the Inland Revenue. Mr M was a farmer who worked on family lands of about 24 acres, producing mainly rice paddy.

In the hearing, Miss D said that she had come to Britain as a young child in 1979. She had always been teased that she was going to marry the appellant in childhood. After she completed her A-levels, she was told that she would be going to Bangladesh to get married. She had agreed, but after the marriage had suffered health problems, and returned to Britain. She now wanted her husband to join her since she felt unable to live in Bangladesh.

She described how this came about in her examination-in-chief:

R: **So how long before you left this country, about how long were you formally told [about the arranged marriage]?**

W: **I was formally told about a year ago.**

A: **[writing] You mean a year before you went.**

W: **Yes, a year before I went. In 1993, before my exams they said they were planning to take me. I said 'fine'. I had no problems in accepting that.**

A: **Right.**

R: **So what did you say when they told you about the marriage?**

W: **My mother asked me and I said to her I came here when I was two-and-a-half years old, and I had reservations about Bangladesh. I have never been back and the climate's really hot. I said I'd go over there, get married, and if I adjust to it, there's nothing to stop me settling. If I don't like it, I'll come back and call my husband over.**

[ ]

R: So, after you reached Bangladesh, how did you find it?

W: Well, from the moment I arrived, I got really ill. I got ill even before the marriage, so obviously I got a bad feeling about the country. I was getting boils, diarrhoea, everything from fever to stomach aches.

The Entry Clearance Officer had refused the application for Mr M to join his wife on a number of grounds which are summarised in the adjudicator's determination. These included:

"... the appellant's acceptance of the first proposal of marriage made to him by a UK resident; the appellant's claimed ignorance as to whether or not the question of residence had been discussed during the marriage negotiations; the failure to provide medical evidence to support the appellant's claim that his wife had returned to the UK four weeks after the wedding because of boils; the comparatively short time that the couple had lived together; [and the] history of migration in the family (his uncle, sister, and a brother live in the UK)."

The Entry Clearance Officer, because of these, and other factors, refused to believe that the sponsor's 'Londini' status was not the primary purpose behind the marriage.

Most of the questions put to Miss D during her examination-in-chief and cross-examination concerned the circumstances of the arranged marriage. The Presenting Officer, for example, wanted to know why she was prepared to 'break with tradition' by not joining her husband's household. However, the adjudicator also seemed concerned to establish why she was willing to marry the appellant, when she had grown up in the West:

A: You have basically been brought up in this country Miss D. I don't know what you do in the Inland Revenue but you are obviously an intelligent sophisticated young lady. Did it never occur to you that it would be strange taking on somebody from a totally different environment?

W: Well, we are from the same family, and just because he's class seven [a grade similar to GCSE level in the Bangladeshi educational system] I don't see any difficulty. There's no

> **difficulty in communication, and because we're from the same family, it didn't matter. I was marrying into the same family, the same house. I had no difficulty with that. It never bothered me really.**

This was another appeal which the adjudicator said that he would allow at the end of the hearing. The determination states that he was completely convinced by the evidence given by Miss D, and could not "really see why the Entry Clearance Officer took the adverse view that he did of this marriage". He also felt that the argument about breaking with tradition was no longer relevant:

> **"I do, however, accept that the appellant will be almost certainly better off if he is able to come to this country, and that it is customary for a wife to join her husband. In my view, the economic factor was not the main object or primary purpose behind this marriage, and there are perfectly good reasons why in this case the British sponsor should wish to call her husband to join her in this country. This particular tradition has largely broken down, certainly where cross-border marriages are concerned."**

Appeal 3

The appellant was an Indian woman, Miss E, who was seeking to enter the United Kingdom as the fiancée of Mr A. The application had been refused in March 1994, and the hearing took place in March 1996.

This marriage had been arranged between two Sikh families, using the services of Mr A's maternal aunt as a matchmaker. An unusual feature of this appeal was that the sponsor had a speech defect, and gave his evidence through a speech therapist who translated his answers. This was significant evidentially in that when she was interviewed by the Entry Clearance Officer, Miss E had given the impression that they communicated normally on the telephone.

I obtained a copy of the interview with the appellant, and it is worth reproducing a section which illustrates the type of questions asked by Entry Clearance Officers. The previous question had established that the family had chosen a matchmaker who lived in the United Kingdom to find a suitable match for Miss E:

16. **Why the UK?**

    It was to my liking to go overseas and settle there.

17. **Why?**

    Because A's maternal aunt loves me very much and treats me as a daughter. I, therefore, wanted to be there.

18. **When parents asked her to look for a match was it a requirement that the boy should live in the UK?**

    My mother's view was he should be of a nice nature and in the UK.

19. **Why not in India?**

    This lady in the UK had already seen the boy so he was arranged for me.

20. **Was it a requirement that your fiancé should live in the UK?**

    Yes, it was mother's wish [sic] that the boy should be from the UK.

21. **But why?**

    I liked her nature and friend's sister [sic] is married in the UK and is also like a sister. There is no other reason.

22. **If this boy lived in India would you have agreed to marry him?**

    Yes, if I liked him I must have married him [sic].

This appeal was also allowed, and in the determination the adjudicator said that he had been impressed by the evidence given by Mr A's mother. She had described how she had first looked for a suitable marriage partner for her son in the United Kingdom without success, and had broken with tradition by allowing the couple to spend time together after the engagement ceremony in India to see how they got on.

On the question of the appellant's intentions (which had to be given most weight in deciding the appeal), he made the following assessment of the answers given during the interview:

"At first sight, there appear to be inconsistencies in that evidence. However, a careful reading of the questions and answers shows that, while the appellant's mother may well have intended her to marry someone from the United Kingdom, she herself wished to marry the sponsor and more than once said clearly that she would have accepted him even if he lived in India. Weighing up these points, and although I have no direct evidence of her mother's intentions, it must, from the recorded interview, be at least open to question whether her primary concern was for her daughter to marry in the United Kingdom. I am, however, satisfied, on a balance of probabilities, that the appellant agreed to the match because she liked and wished to marry the boy regardless of where he lived."

Appeal 4

This appellant was a Pakistani man, Mr S, who was seeking to enter the country to join his wife, following their arranged marriage in 1995. The appeal was heard in November 1996.

The Entry Clearance Officer refused the application partly because of discrepancies between the interviews given by the appellant and the sponsor. They had, for example, given different accounts about when the match was arranged, and when it had been decided to live in the United Kingdom. Differences in their answers about the age of different cousins suggested to the Entry Clearance Officer that there had been an attempt to 'prune' the family tree: in other words, to conceal the existence of eligible cousins in Pakistan who were of marriageable age.

The appellant in this appeal was represented by a barrister who spent a considerable amount of time reviewing the law in his closing submission. At one point, he became involved in a disagreement with the adjudicator:

R: **On the point of breaches with tradition, see the case of *ex parte Walle* (1989, page 86), a fiancé case. You'll see on page 91....**

A: **[Looks a little impatient] Yes, OK, I am familiar with this.**

R: **It says there is no reason on earth why a British citizen should not insist that her fiancé should not have her live in Asia.**

> Sir, the next step on the way is [ ] in Immigration Court Practice. It was held that in marriage cases, *Walle* is binding on adjudicators and no adverse conclusions should be drawn on the imposition of a conclusion.

A: I may say that, in *Walle*, I, of course, have taken notice that the case continues, and that there is a bit there that is less helpful to you.

B: I can go through it.

A: No, I'm saying you can spot-pick the section that favours you.

B: Well, I'm saying it's the ratio of the case. Perhaps your case is the case of *Masood* which says it's not relevant [ ].

A: I'm not going to have an argument, but I think it's a purposive interpretation of the rule. These are all cases about the substantive question you raised earlier. What is the primary purpose of the marriage in [ ], *Hoque and Singh*, and other cases? You don't need to go through these with me.

B: Can I just ask you to look at a long passage from *Safter*?

This attempt to construct a legal argument around the authorities was considered inappropriate because the principles in this area of law had been agreed. However, Mr S still won the appeal, despite the discrepancies in the evidence, because the adjudicator accepted the account given by the sponsor.

Appeal 5

This was the appeal of a Pakistani man, Mr W, against a refusal of entry clearance to join his wife, following their traditional arranged marriage in March 1994. It was heard in May 1996.

Before the hearing, the counsellor told me that this was a 'middle of the road' case, in that there were a number of problems in her evidence which might lead some adjudicators to dismiss the appeal.

The first of these was the fact that there had been two breaches with cultural tradition, which the Home Office could use to suggest that the primary purpose had been to gain entry for the husband to the United

Kingdom. In a traditional marriage, the wife was expected to live with her husband's family. It was also normal for first cousins to marry, whereas the couple in this case were second cousins.

In her examination-in-chief, the counsellor sought to demonstrate that there were acceptable reasons for the applicant not marrying a first cousin:

C: **Does your husband have first cousins in Pakistan?**

S: **Yes.**

C: **Why did he not get married to a first cousin in Pakistan?**

S: **They're either married, or they're too young for him. He's only got two who are younger than him and the rest are married.**

C: **And did he have second cousins whom he could get married to in Pakistan?**

S: **He didn't get on well with them. He had family problems.**

C: **What problems?**

S: **Family problems.**

C: **Who were these second cousins he could have married?**

S: **My mum's sister's daughters.**

C: **And what family problems did they have?**

S: **They just don't get on. They're really apart. My mum and dad have got a really good relationship [with them] as first cousins. They're only related to them. They're not really close.**

There were, however, no special circumstances to justify breaking with the tradition that a wife should go and live with her husband's family. Instead, the sponsor told the court that she did not consider herself bound by this tradition:

C: **What about this tradition the Entry Clearance Officer talks about in paragraph 6 – once a woman gets married, she has to join her husband in his country?**

> S: The traditions I like, I go along with them. The traditions
>   I don't like, I don't take much notice of them.

A second problem was that the sponsor and her husband differed in their accounts of how the marriage had been arranged. According to the sponsor, she had told her mother that she would only live in the United Kingdom before the wedding. The appellant, however, told the Entry Clearance Officer that this had not been decided before the wedding. Matters were made worse, from the perspective of the counsellor, when the two witnesses she called – the sponsor and her father – unexpectedly gave conflicting accounts of how the marriage had been arranged. The counsellor told me later that this kind of discrepancy could be extremely damaging. It suggested that the whole truth had not been told to the court, and some adjudicators might feel that this included the real intentions behind the marriage.

Two further problems that concerned the counsellor were the quality of the evidence about the issues of 'intervening devotion' and 'maintenance and accommodation'. She knew, from experience, that this appeal could be dismissed on either of these grounds. In the event, the adjudicator allowed the appeal. In his determination, he ignored the issue of 'breach with tradition', and accepted the sponsor's version of events. He did, however, make it clear that the appellant had only just discharged the burden of proof:

> "In my view, this is a very marginal case. The appellant has not helped himself by producing documentary evidence to support his appeal, but, on the totality of the evidence before me, the balance has, just, tipped in favour of the appellant, and thus I consider that sub-paragraph (a) has been satisfied."

Appeal 6

This was the appeal of an Indian woman, Mrs F, seeking to join her husband in the United Kingdom after an arranged marriage that had taken place in 1994. The hearing took place in October 1996.

This sponsor was 46 years old and had been married before. He worked as an engineer at Heathrow airport. The appellant was in her mid-30s (the court had no record of her exact date of birth), and had a university degree. Her family had started looking for an arranged marriage when she was 28.

In her interview, the appellant said that her family had been trying to arrange a marriage for two or three years, and that she had seen '10 or 12 boys' in the Punjab who were not suitable. In her summary of the facts, the adjudicator noted:

> "Local boys had been disregarded by the appellant's family because of their lack of property or education, and it was found to be significant that they were then willing to accept a match with a man 14 years older than the appellant and who had two children from his first marriage. It was also noted that the marriage was agreed before the sponsor's divorce decree absolute came through and a man in these circumstances would not normally be considered a good match in India."

In her interview, the appellant told the Entry Clearance Officer that the only thing she knew about the sponsor, before the match was agreed, was that he was from the United Kingdom, had a good job, and did not drink. She did not know the reasons why his marriage had failed, or the names of his children.

The sponsor told the court that he had been looking for a wife since his divorce, but had no success in the United Kingdom. He had seen three or four girls he did not like, but he immediately liked his wife, and had asked her to marry him on their first meeting in 1993. He had since been to India many times, and stayed with his wife for two or three weeks on each visit. He telephoned more than once a week, and also wrote, although he had not kept any of the letters they had exchanged.

The submissions in this appeal are worth reproducing to show how the two sides constructed a case out of the evidence presented to the court. They are both typical of closing statements, although some representatives spent more time reviewing the facts, and discussing the relevant law.

The Home Office Presenting Officer made the following submission:

> H: **Maam, I'd rely in part on the Entry Clearance Officer's explanatory statement. I would ask you to note there are discrepancies between the appellant's and sponsor's account of their first meeting. According to the sponsor, they met alone, and the appellant agreed to marry on the**

first meeting. Maam, if the appellant is not telling the truth, I suggest there can only be an intention to deceive the Entry Clearance Officer to try to suggest that this was not a speedy arrangement for marriage.

Because the obvious conclusion, if the marriage was agreed after one brief meeting, is that the sponsor's UK status was the factor that made the marriage agreeable to the family.

I would ask you to note that the sponsor [will not] move to India if this appeal fails. I would ask you to note that this marriage is conditional on entry clearance.

I would refer you to the case of *Masood*, unfortunately I don't have the reference.

A: That's OK.

H: In all the circumstances, I would ask you to find the primary purpose was for coming to the UK. I would ask you to note there is no evidence of intervening devotion in the bundle. The sponsor was not able to give her telephone number, so there is no evidence of intervening devotion. I would ask you to dismiss the appeal.

The appellant was represented by a counsellor from the Immigration Advisory Service:

"Maam, I'd ask you to find this a properly arranged marriage, done in the proper way between the parties.

Maam, I'd ask you to find that even if this was not the best marriage, the appellant's family were not strictly traditional themselves. They had educated their daughter to degree level, and she was also above marriageable age. I would submit that knowledge of economic benefits does not necessarily mean there was a primary purpose to enter the UK. The fact she turned down suitors is understandable because she is far more educated than the suitors she mentions, and can't be expected to marry a totally uneducated person.

Maam, the discrepancies, I would suggest, arose because both parties had decided on marriage before the decree absolute had come through and did not want to fall foul of the ECO. This shows why the discrepancies arose. These discrepancies do not show a primary intent to enter the UK, and should not be treated as important.

I would ask you to note that the Home Office have not queried the appellant or sponsor's credibility [   ].

I would ask you to note that the primary purpose of the marriage was to find a husband for the appellant, not to gain entry into the UK. I would ask you to note that the wife [ ] goes to where her husband is settled, so there is nothing unconventional in arranging this marriage.

I would also ask you to see this is an arranged marriage, and should not be judged by Western standards. The appellant married because of the sponsor's education and life-style, not because of getting entry status.

Finally, I'd ask you to allow this appeal.

In her determination, the adjudicator accepted the submission of the Home Office:

"It is my finding that the appellant agreed to the match even before the sponsor's decree absolute was announced, and knowing very little about him, because it was her primary purpose in marrying him to enter the United Kingdom where her prospects and standard of living as an educated woman would be much improved. I, therefore, conclude that her application does not comply with the immigration rules.

The appeal is dismissed."

Some methodological issues

Before discussing these six case studies, it is important to recognise their limitations as data. Each of the determinations runs to about seven A4-

size pages of single-spaced type, so the extracts I have supplied provide only a small part of the adjudicator's summary of the evidence presented in the hearings. The transcripts I have presented similarly provide only a selective illustration of what took place in court.

There are, of course, a number of ways in which one can respond to this kind of data. Some sociologists might complain that I have already provided too much detail about what took place in hearings, or that I should have been more selective in presenting a corpus of data about a particular aspect of decision making. Many researchers in the interpretive tradition would, however, suggest that I have not gone far enough in preserving the phenomenon I wish to address as an analyst[4]. It might be argued, for example, that I should place the full transcripts of the six hearings, along with copies of all the documents I was able to obtain, on a website for public inspection and analysis[5].

Whether or not preserving full hearings for analysis is practicable or desirable, I would want to suggest that, while these case studies clearly have their limitations as data, they do provide access to the kind of issues that concerned practitioners which are not usually preserved in sociological or sociolinguistic studies of the courtroom. They are, therefore, useful for my purposes in addressing the practical content of legal work which might not interest other analysts.

Finally, it is worth noting that, in discussing these cases, I have little interest in evaluating how these decisions were made (see, for example, Peay, 1989), even though I could have attempted to write my own determination after each appeal, based on my own understanding of the facts and law[6]. This is because it is impossible to recreate all the evidence presented in even one appeal in the pages of a sociological study. Instead of evaluating how adjudicators made decisions, I will instead focus on the manner in which they assessed different types of evidence.

Decision making in primary purpose appeals

The key question an adjudicator had to determine in this kind of appeal was whether a marriage had been entered into primarily to gain entry to the United Kingdom. This can be illustrated by considering the evidential issues raised by the Filipino appeal in my sample, and the five Asian arranged marriage cases.

Demonstrating love for an older man

In Appeal 1, the couple had to demonstrate they had fallen in love, rather than that Miss C was interested in a man 30 years older than herself because he lived in the United Kingdom. Here the factors that led the Entry Clearance Officer to refuse Miss C's application included the age difference, and her standard of living in the Philippines relative to the United Kingdom[7].

There were two significant factors in Miss C's favour in this appeal. The first had been her conduct during the relationship. The court was told, for example, that she had refused to come to England on a visit, until her immigration status had been resolved, and that she had supported Mr R through a serious illness. The second was that Mr R impressed the adjudicator as a witness (and the representative also described him as "not a gullible sponsor"). The fact he had been in the army made it possible for him to be categorised as someone who was a good judge of people and "knows the ways of men and women".

This illustrates how adjudicators employed the kind of common-sense knowledge that everyone has, through belonging to a particular culture, about the genuineness of a relationship, although it is also worth noting that another adjudicator could just as well have reached a different decision on the same set of facts. The fact the adjudicator gave the result on the spot indicated that he believed that this appellant had a particularly strong case.

Demonstrating the genuineness of an arranged marriage

In the case of Asian appellants, the first task of adjudicators was to establish if this was a properly arranged traditional marriage. In Pakistan and Bangladesh, it was common for marriages to be made between first cousins. In India, families would often employ the services of a matchmaker. The question then arose, however, as to whether the primary purpose of these marriages was to enter the United Kingdom. Here, adjudicators differed in the tests they used, and the weight they gave different factors. My case studies illustrate the importance of six types of evidence.

Intervening devotion

The Court of Appeal in *Kumar* had suggested that evidence of 'intervening devotion' in the form of letters, or visits, could 'throw a flood of light' on the primary purpose of a marriage. This was an important factor behind the favourable decision in Appeals 2 to 5. Letters were produced to the court, and also tapes which had been exchanged between the parties. In Appeal 5, one problem for the counsellor was that the evidence of 'intervening devotion' was poor. The adjudicator noted that the expression of devotion in one letter appeared to have been made for the purpose of obtaining a favourable outcome in the appeal.

The appellant's interview

The record made by the Entry Clearance Officer of the interview with the appellant was an important document that the adjudicator considered in making a decision. There were always some discrepancies between the answers of the sponsor and appellant. In the case of serious differences, the representative could usually challenge the way in which the interview had been conducted. In Appeal 4, the barrister suggested that the sponsor and appellant had got up very early to travel to Islamabad for their interview, and had been given no refreshments. They had then been asked 'leading questions'. The adjudicator agreed that the officer conducting the interview had not given them sufficient time to elaborate on their answers. However, he felt they had no right to complain about their early start, since they could easily have made arrangements to stay overnight in Islamabad[8].

Breaches with cultural tradition

One issue raised by all the Entry Clearance Officers in these appeals was that there had been a 'breach of tradition' which indicated that the primary purpose of the marriage was to come to the United Kingdom. These traditions included the fact that women should normally join their husbands after a marriage, and that Pakistani and Bangladeshi marriages should normally be arranged between first cousins. The sponsor in Appeal 5 had, therefore, to explain to the court why she was marrying a second cousin. The ages of different cousins could also become an issue, as in Appeal 3, in that a couple had to show that there were no suitable marriage partners in their own countries.

None of these adjudicators placed any weight on the fact there had been a breach with cultural tradition in their determinations. The Court of Appeal in *Kumar* had advised Entry Clearance Officers to disregard this as a factor in deciding the primary purpose of a marriage.

Representatives could not, however, be sure what line any particular adjudicator would take on the matter.

It is worth noting that the issue of breaches with tradition was often used by those advocating more restrictive immigration controls in the 1970s and 1980s. A standard argument was that the courts had a duty to respect the cultural traditions of other countries (such as the tradition that wives should join their husbands), just as immigrants should respect our cultural traditions.

The eligibility of the partners

It has been suggested that some applications were refused in the 1980s because Entry Clearance Officers considered that an applicant had married, or wished to marry, a less physically attractive sponsor, with the aim of getting entry to the United Kingdom. The one appeal in this sample which was refused involved an older divorced man who had married a younger woman in India. However, in Appeal 3, a woman was allowed to join her husband in the United Kingdom, despite the fact that he had a speech impediment.

The arrangements for the marriage

There was a considerable amount of evidence presented in each of these hearings about how the marriage had been arranged, and in particular whether it had been decided that the appellant would live in the United Kingdom before the wedding. As in the case of breaches of tradition, recent cases had decided that it was proper for a fiancé to make it a condition for entering into the marriage that the couple would live in Britain. However, it appears that none of these appellants wanted to admit this. Instead, the sponsor in Appeal 2 told the court that she had agreed to live in India, but that the hot climate forced her to return to Britain. In Appeal 4, the appellant was quite open about the constricting nature of life as a woman in rural Pakistan, where it was not possible to go to the shops without being veiled and in the company of a male relative.

The appellant's standard of living

Another factual issue raised by the Entry Clearance Officer in most of these appeals was the standard of living of the appellant. Invariably, the sponsor told the court that the appellant's family were well-off by the standards of their own country. There was no economic motive to marry someone from the United Kingdom.

This evidence was summarised in the determinations, but not commented on by adjudicators. One reason for this may have been that the Scottish Court of Session decided in *Safter* that an economic motive to enter the United Kingdom did not in itself prove that this was the primary purpose of the marriage. However, it seems clear that the assumption behind the rule was that a major reason for this type of secondary migration was the perception among Asian families that there were economic advantages to living in Britain.

The role of judicial sympathy

In terms of law, the intentions of the sponsor were of only secondary relevance in an arranged marriage. The key factor to consider was the intention of the families who had arranged it. Even if an adjudicator felt that the parents of the appellant had been trying to find a partner in the United Kingdom, a 'good' sponsor could still turn the appeal around for the appellant.

This raises the issue of whether cultural prejudice operated in another way in that some adjudicators may have used the law to protect 'vulnerable' sponsors. It is interesting, for example, that the adjudicator asked if the sponsor was happy to enter into the arranged marriage in three of these appeals. Women sometimes handed in notes, before the hearing, asking the court to find against the appellant.

Adjudicators were expected to make decisions without being influenced by any cultural prejudices they might have against the arranged marriage system. I met one adjudicator who was quite open about the fact he did have such a prejudice, but that this did not affect his ability to apply the law to the facts of any particular appeal. It is worth supplying a long extract from this interview, since I would imagine that many readers will hold similar ethnocentric views:

> **"I don't like – and I don't like having to say this, because I live in an Asian area, and some of my best friends are Asian – I don't like the arranged marriage system. The daughters of Hindus, Muslims and Sikhs are expected to be married by age 17. It doesn't mean that they get married then. They are forced to take a husband from the Indian subcontinent who have much lower educational standards than themselves....**

Is it right that, in Pakistan, girls look to their first cousins to marry? This is genetically not good. I saw a television programme on this, and it doubles their infant mortality rate by the age of 10, therefore you get these inbred communities. Should we be encouraging that situation where people who are British, and who have every right and opportunity, are pushed to marry someone in Pakistan, who, it is clear, knows nothing about the girl?

Therefore, I have a cultural prejudice. The law is 'Was it the primary purpose of the couple to live in the UK?', and this is a difficult thing to decide. I often find that I have a really nice girl, highly articulate and intelligent. Last week it was a Sikh girl. I felt very sorry for her. She said that she couldn't find a husband in England because she was dark-skinned – if so that's an example of racism in the Asian community – and because she is the sort of person who is an asset. I thought that she had convinced herself that her husband was in love with her, but it was clear from the interview that he couldn't give a damn.

I was going to give her the appeal. You know how you form a preliminary view. The primary purpose of the appellant was marriage – the sponsor's view only has to be taken into account – but when I read the interview, it was clear he didn't give a damn. He was off-hand. The Entry Clearance Officer nearly stopped the interview because he was giving off-hand cheeky replies....

No decision that you make will be free of people's personal attitudes and predilections. Except that in this case, it was obvious from the interview that he was going over to marry for economic reasons."

The significance of the primary purpose rule

According to Sachdeva (1993, p 90), the primary purpose rule became the main device used to refuse entry to spouses and fiancés from Asian countries during the 1980s. Critics of the rule complained that it became difficult, if not impossible, to win an appeal, since the appellant had to prove a negative (that the primary purpose of the marriage was *not* to enter the United Kingdom). Bhabha et al (1985) note that the refusal rate jumped from between 4% and 10% between 1977 and 1981, to over 40% after 1982. In 1984, 47% of husbands and male fiancées were refused because of the rule. Statistics were not kept by the Home Office after the late 1980s, but according to the most recent edition of the Joint Council for the Welfare of Immigrants (JCWI) Handbook, only 20% of all non-asylum appeals in 1995 were successful in the courts.

A rather different picture was presented to me by practitioners during my fieldwork. According to counsellors working for the IAS, there were far fewer primary purpose appeals, as a result of the 1992 concession, and they were winning more and more of these cases[9]. Presenting Officers also recognised that the rule 'was on its way out', since it was likely that there would eventually be a successful challenge in the European courts. There was, therefore, no great surprise among practitioners when the Labour government announced that it was planning to abolish the rule.

My six case studies, which may, of course, be unrepresentative of the thousands of appeals heard each year by different adjudicators across the country, indicate that appellants who could show that they had a traditionally arranged marriage were usually successful. On the other hand, Entry Clearance Officers were still able to dismiss many applications, which resulted in long delays for couples affected by the rule.

How one understands the significance of the primary purpose rule, ultimately, depends on making a political judgement about immigration control. For critics, the rule was unfair towards individuals, and was intended not simply to restrict further immigration from Asia, but also to force Asian immigrants and their families to assimilate. Sachdeva (1993, p 92) notes that the relatively small Asian population in the United Kingdom meant that families were forced to look overseas for marriage partners for their children. British policy, therefore, seemed designed to prevent Asian women finding husbands, or to engineer the break-up of the community by forcing them to marry outside their own ethnic group.

Appellants themselves viewed the rule as unfair, since it prevented them from following tradition, or marrying the partner of their choice. I also met young Asians who were quite open about the fact that there was an economic motive behind the entire arranged marriage system. In appeals hearings, however, it was necessary to persuade the court that this was not the primary purpose of the marriage.

For the politicians who supported tougher immigration controls on marriages during the 1970s and early 1980s, the primary purpose rule must appear as a successful measure that reduced, or at least postponed, immigration from the Asian subcontinent to Britain. Here, it might be noted, that Britain's obligations to allow family reunion under international law made it impossible to sustain strict controls. It is still unclear whether significant numbers will continue to gain entry to Britain through arranged marriages, and whether they will continue to be refused under the provisions in the rules about 'intention to live together' and 'maintenance and accommodation'. Anyone who admits that their main reason for marriage is to live in the United Kingdom is now entitled to do so under British immigration law.

Notes

[1] See the decision of the European Court of Human Rights in *Abdulaziz, Cabales and Balkandali v UK*, reported at [1985] 7 EHRR 471.

[2] The full references for the cases discussed in this section are: *Arun Kumar* [1986] ImmAR 446 [CA]; *Vinod Bhatia v Immigration Appeal Tribunal* [1985] ImmAR 50 [CA]; *IAT v Amirul Hoque and Matwinder Singh* [1988] ImmAR 226; *Mohammed Safter v Secretary of State for the Home Department* [1992] ImmAR 1; and *Sumeina Masood* v IAT [1992] ImmAR 69.

[3] See *R v IAT and Surinder Singh ex parte Home Secretary* [1992] ALL ER 798.

[4] Earlier this century, many of the best interpretive studies in America were based upon several years of fieldwork by teams of researchers. One example is Thomas and Znaniecki's (1958) two-volume study of Polish immigration into America. This contains a translation of 40 letters that were exchanged between immigrants and their families, and the 80-page autobiography of a particular immigrant, as well as an analysis of these materials. Publication of this data was itself seen as an important contribution to knowledge by these sociologists. For a discussion of the methodological significance of their work, see Plummer (1983).

[5] This would cause practical difficulties owing to the confidential nature of legal documents. In principle, however, the technology now exists for analysts to publish larger datasets, and also audio- and video-recordings, using the world wide web. For a discussion of methodological issues relating to the ESRC Qualdata Project, which hopes to establish an archive of such materials, see Hammersley (1997).

[6] The televising of criminal trials in America has created a whole industry based on the fact that the public can be given much of the evidence that is available to jurors in reaching a verdict. Public reaction to the O.J. Simpson and Louise

Woodward trials illustrates that the public can interpret the same evidence in dramatically different ways, and tend to support members of their own racial or ethnic group.

[7] Many marriages in Britain also take place for economic reasons, and young women often marry older men, and this is likely to continue so long as most women continue to earn less than most men (Bradley, 1996).

[8] The allegedly aggressive manner in which Entry Clearance Officers conducted some of these interviews, and their assumptions about applicants, attracted considerable criticism from pressure groups and community organisations during the 1970s and 1980s. See, for example, Commission for Racial Equality (1985). Presenting Officers, however, tended to view interviews in a different light. One officer, who had previously worked as an Entry Clearance Officer, believed that adjudicators would refuse more, rather than less, appeals if all interviews were taped. In her view, it was 'obvious' from the demeanour of appellants, and the side-exchanges between them, that they were not telling the truth.

[9] According to one counsellor, this may have been because the numbers of people seeking asylum far outweighed those entering through marriage: it had become a priority to keep these out, which benefited people seeking to enter through marriage.

FIVE

Political asylum and the courts

Whereas the primary purpose rule is now in the past, British policy towards those applying for asylum under the 1951 United Nations Convention on Refugees continues to be a contentious political issue. According to Home Office statistics, an average of 7% of applicants each year were recognised as refugees between 1992 and 1997, although an average of 24% were given Exceptional Leave to Remain[1].

Conservative governments in Britain during the late 1980s and 1990s took the view that most people applying for asylum were, in fact, economic migrants who were using the Convention to gain access to Britain. Although ministers in Tony Blair's New Labour government have made fewer public statements about the 'bogus' character of claims, policy on asylum has not appreciably changed. The numerous organisations and pressure groups representing refugees continue to argue that most claims are genuine, and that adjudicators dismiss too many appeals. Only 4% were successful during the period 1993-96, although this has increased to about 6% since 1997.

My objective in this chapter is not to advance a political argument about the way appeals are decided in the courts, although the data I will be presenting could be used by either side in this debate. Instead, I again want to focus on how practitioners understand legal and evidential issues in the course of their day-to-day work.

I will begin by providing some historical background on the Convention and the process of determining asylum claims in Britain, and present a summary of six appeals from my corpus of data. I will then discuss some general features of decision making, and consider the claim made by organisations representing refugees that their low success rate can be attributed to a 'culture of refusal' in the courts.

The 1951 Convention and British law

The 1951 Convention was signed by 197 countries, as one of a series of agreements, including the formation of the United Nations, that were intended to re-establish and strengthen the international community following the Second World War.

Signatories of the Convention are required to provide protection to anyone satisfying the following definition of a 'refugee' set out in Article 1(A):

> **For the purposes of the present Convention, the term 'refugee' shall apply to any person who ... as a result of events occurring before 1 January 1951 and owing to a well-founded fear of being persecuted for reasons of race, religion, nationality, membership of a particular social group or political opinion, is outside the country of his nationality and is unable or, owing to such fear, is unwilling to avail himself of the protection of that country....**

In a 1967 Protocol, contracting states agreed to remove the limitation to 'events occurring before 1 January 1951'. Article 1(B) of the Convention gave them the opportunity to make a declaration limiting the events that produced the fear of persecution to Europe, and this right was preserved in the 1967 Protocol. All countries in the West do, however, give protection to anyone who, according to their own procedures, is recognised as a refugee under Article 1(A), irrespective of their country of origin. The Office of the United Nations High Commissioner for Refugees was established in 1951 and monitors how signatories are fulfilling their obligations. It has no powers to issue sanctions, and the Convention itself does not specify the legal arrangements that states should adopt in determining refugee status. The British office is on the 21st floor of Millbank Tower on the embankment, overlooking the Houses of Parliament[2].

Many academic commentators now criticise the Convention for only affording protection to a narrow class of people who can show that they have been persecuted for a Convention reason (see, for example, Tuitt, 1996). People who have fled from their own states owing to war or natural disaster cannot, for example, claim to be Convention refugees. In the context of the immediate post-war period, it was intended to provide protection to ethnic groups like the Jews who had been displaced in large numbers from their own countries following persecution by the Nazis. It was also used by Western states to protect dissidents who had defected from the Soviet Union, or its satellite states in Eastern Europe, during the Cold War.

The rise of the 'new asylum-seeker' in the 1980s

In the late 1980s, governments across the developed world were surprised by a dramatic rise in the number of people claiming asylum[3]. The "new asylum-seekers" (Joly and Cohen, 1989) mainly came from Africa, Asia, Latin America and the Middle East. There have also, however, been increasing numbers of people claiming asylum from Europe. In 1995, 43,965 applications were made for asylum in Britain, from the following countries[4]:

(A) ASIA (24%)
Afghanistan 580; China 790; India 3,255; Pakistan 2,915; Sri Lanka 2,070; Other 1,075.
Total: 10,685

(B) AFRICA (51%)
Algeria 1,865; Angola 555; Ethiopia 585; Gambia 1,170; Ghana 1,915; Ivory Coast 245; Kenya 1,395; Liberia 390; Nigeria 5,825; Sierra Leone 855; Somalia 3,465; Sudan 345; Tanzania 1,535; Togo 75; Uganda 365; Zaïre 935; Other 1,030.
Total: 22,550

(C) MIDDLE EAST (5%)
Iran 615; Iraq 930; Lebanon 150; Other 600.
Total: 2,295

(D) THE AMERICAS (3%)
Columbia 525; Other 815.
Total: 1,340

(E) EUROPE (16%)
Bulgaria 480; Cyprus 200; Poland 1,210; Romania 770; Turkey 1,820; Former USSR 795; Former Yugoslavia 1,565; Other 215.
Total: 7,055

This rise in the numbers seeking protection has been attributed to the fact that there has been more instability inside states in the world system, and especially in the Third World, in the post-war period, and that cheap air travel now makes it possible to travel across the globe relatively easily (Mortimer, 1996). Western governments have, however, been suspicious about the claims made by these 'new asylum-seekers', viewing many as economic migrants. It has been argued, from this perspective, that people who wish to migrate to the West, for a variety of reasons, have discovered that claiming asylum is an effective means of circumventing immigration controls.

The recognition of refugees in Britain

Only a tiny number of people claimed asylum in Britain during the 1960s, and it was not thought necessary to include a section on the Convention in the 1971 Immigration Act. There were provisions about asylum-seekers in the immigration rules issued by the Home Office from the late 1960s, but according to MacDonald and Blake, the primacy of the 1971 Act meant that many asylum-seekers only had a limited right of appeal to the courts:

> **People who claimed asylum after they arrived in the UK and were given a leave to enter had a right of appeal to an adjudicator against a refusal, but those who claimed asylum on arrival were limited to judicial review until they were removed to the place of feared persecution. (MacDonald and Blake 1995, p 378)**

The large numbers claiming asylum in the late 1980s led most Western states to review their procedures for recognising Convention refugees. The response of the British government was the 1993 Asylum and Immigration Act which gave all asylum-seekers a right of appeal to 'special adjudicators' in the immigration courts.

In contrast to the slow and uncertain development of case-law on the primary purpose rule, an early decision by the House of Lords in the 1988 case of *Sivakumaran* established the test that is used in determining whether there is a 'well-founded fear' in asylum appeals[5].

According to Sir John Donaldson in the Court of Appeal, the Home Office had erred in law by using its own knowledge of conditions in Sri Lanka to assess whether the applicants had a 'well-founded fear'. Instead, they should have applied the following subjective test:

> **"Authority apart, we would accept that 'well-founded' fear is demonstrated by proving (a) actual fear and (b) good reason for this fear, looking at the situation from the point of view of one of reasonable courage.... Fear is clearly an entirely subjective**

state experienced by the person who is afraid. The adjectival phrase 'well-founded' qualifies, but cannot transform, the subjective nature of the emotion. The qualification will exclude fears which can be dismissed as paranoid, but we do not understand why it should exclude those which, although fully justified on the face of the situation as it presented itself to the person who was afraid, can be shown objectively to have been misconceived."

Lord Keith of Kinkel, and four other Law Lords, disagreed with this construction of the Convention, on the grounds that it could never have been intended to extend protection to those with fears that were not 'objectively justified'. They suggested instead that the Home Office should assess a claim for asylum in the light of the latest information it had about conditions in that country:

"The question is what might happen if [the claimant to refugee status] were to return to the country of his nationality. He fears that he might be persecuted there. Whether that might happen can only be determined by examining the actual state of affairs in that country. If that examination shows that persecution might indeed take place then the fear is well-founded. Otherwise it is not."

This established the test which continues to be used in deciding asylum appeals. An appellant has to show that they have a subjective fear of persecution, and this has to be 'well-founded' on the basis of the objective circumstances in that country as understood by the court. The burden of proof, which was also decided by this case, is that an applicant must satisfy the Home Office that there is a 'reasonable likelihood' that they will be persecuted. According to one of the authorities approved by the House of Lords, even if there was 'only a 10% chance of being shot, tortured or otherwise persecuted', this would still be a 'well-founded fear'[6]. This can be contrasted with the higher standard of proof in non-asylum appeals in which applicants have to prove an entitlement to enter under the immigration rules on the balance of probabilities; in other words, that there is a 50% chance of their account being true.

Common reasons for refusing refugees

Most asylum appeals are refused for the following reasons.

Jurisdictional objections

The Convention requires refugees to seek asylum in the first safe country they reach. If, therefore, an applicant has travelled through a 'safe third country', the application will be refused by the Home Office as 'without foundation'. The 1993 Act gave a right of appeal to applications dismissed for this reason under what is known as the 'fast-track' procedure. The 1996 Act removed the right to a hearing before removal.

No Convention reason

The narrow way in which persecution has been defined under the Convention means that many applicants fail to establish a legal right to claim asylum, even if the court believes their account of what took place in their own country. One cannot, for example, claim asylum simply through being the victim of a civil war because this is not persecution by reason of 'race, religion, nationality, membership of a particular social group or political opinion'.

Even if an appellant has been a victim of persecution, there are a number of reasons why they may not qualify as a Convention refugee. According to the UNHCR handbook, the persecution needs to come from the state, or 'agents of the state', or to have arisen through the collapse of state power in a particular country (MacDonald and Blake, 1995, p 390). There must also be nowhere in the country where the appellant could reasonably be expected to move which could offer protection from the persecution (this is described in the handbook as the option of 'internal flight').

No subjective fear

Many appeals fail simply because adjudicators do not believe that the appellant has a subjective fear of persecution. In the language used in determinations, the appellant is found to be lacking in 'credibility'; in ordinary language, the adjudicator believes that the appellant is lying, and that no persecution has actually taken place.

No objective circumstances

Even if an adjudicator believes the evidence presented in court, they may still find that the appellant's fear is not 'well-founded'. This may simply be because political circumstances have changed: the government doing the persecuting is, for example, no longer in power. For this reason, part of the task of the adjudicator is to make an up-to-date assessment of the objective circumstances in the appellant's country of nationality, drawing upon documentary evidence supplied by representatives.

Six asylum appeals

To understand why so few appellants are recognised as refugees, it is necessary to examine how these general grounds for refusal become relevant in the circumstances of particular cases. In the rest of this chapter, I will, therefore, be presenting an ethnographic account of six appeals. In each case, I made a contemporaneous note of the hearing, and was also able to obtain a copy of the determination, and sometimes other relevant documents.

Before presenting this data, three caveats are necessary. The first is that it necessarily only gives a taste of the kind of evidence presented to adjudicators in the thousands of appeals which are heard by these courts in any one year. The appellants in these hearings came from the Sudan, Croatia, Turkey, Sri Lanka, Zaïre and the Ivory Coast. However, on each day during my fieldwork, there were appeals from people seeking asylum from many different countries around the world.

The second caveat is that, like the data I presented in the previous chapter about primary purpose appeals, my summaries only provide a fraction of the evidence put before the adjudicator, and might favour one side or the other when taken out of the total context of the evidence presented during the hearing.

A third caveat is that I do not know the outcome of Appeals 3 and 5, since the Immigration Appellate Authority were unable to locate the determinations in their records[7]. However, despite their limitations as data, these summaries reveal a great deal about how adjudicators and representatives understood the legal and evidential issues in these appeals.

Appeal I

This was an appeal by a middle-aged Sudanese couple Mr and Mrs L, and their children, who were seeking asylum on the grounds that they had a 'well-founded fear of persecution' if they were returned to the Sudan. They arrived separately in Britain in 1993, having obtained visas to enter as visitors for six months, and claimed asylum one month later. The appeal was heard in March 1997.

The facts in this appeal were not at issue. Mr L worked for an international relief organisation in the Sudan, and had a good standard of living. He had a company car and a driver, and his employer sent a watchman to his home when he was out of the country on business. However, he and his wife had suffered harassment on a number of occasions from Muslim fundamentalists through being Christians.

Mr L told the court that, shortly after he had sacked a Muslim employee, he received a visit from the security services. He was told that they would be watching him, and that he should report for an interview at 8.00 am the next day at their headquarters. When Mr L arrived for the interview, he was kept waiting in the reception area the whole day, without being able to leave the room, and was then told to report the next day. The same thing happened for the next two days. On the third day, he was called into a room, in which there was an officer sitting "with his legs on top of the table and his shoes facing the door", and questioned about the work of the relief agency, and the help it had given to Christians in southern Sudan.

Mr L explained, through the interpreter, that "the culture or custom when you see someone with their shoes pointing at you is a sign of disrespect". In the security office, and also on the street, he was always called 'kafiq'. This meant 'unbeliever', but "it also means I am untouchable or diseased. It is a humiliation".

Although he could practise his religion in private by going to church, he was required to work on Sundays since the Sudan was a Muslim country. He also felt that it was unwise to wear a crucifix in public. He reported how:

> **"On one occasion while I was in the security office, I had a gold chain with a cross round my neck inside my shirt, and accidentally the cross appeared through the shirt buttons. Immediately, the security men grabbed hold of the cross and pulled it, broke the chain, and threw it on the ground. And**

then he pressed his shoe, stepped on the cross, and told me you
musn't wear the cross in public."

Mrs L told the court that the family had just moved into a new house in
a predominantly Muslim area, and she had become afraid of her
neighbours. To begin with she had received a visit from "veiled women"
who wanted to know if she was a Christian, which they suspected because
of the colour of her skin, and the fact that the landlord "came from the
South". She described how she met these women outside the house
when she went shopping:

> W: ... on my way to the shop, they demanded from me that
> I must cover my hair as it is an Islamic country. And at
> that time I was wearing respectable clothes. I was dressed
> in trousers, but did not cover my head. The way they
> demanded of me they said it in the manner of a warning
> or a threat.
>
> A few days later I again went out to the shop. The same
> way as I was dressed before. I was followed by two veiled
> women. One of them approached me from the back and
> pulled me from my hair. And the other grabbed my
> clothes. They both told me that we have already told you
> that you must cover your hair. I told them that I was a
> Christian. At the time, I was frightened and stressful.
> After that I was very frightened to go out shopping again.
> I only went out when I was desperate to go to the shops.
>
> R: Did you report this to the police?
>
> W: I personally did not because I am a wife. The wife doesn't
> take any action. Usually the husband should take the
> action, and besides that I was newly resident in the area.

Two further things had occurred which made her fearful about remaining
in the Sudan. The first was that her children were beaten up at school,
and when they went out to the shop, and on one occasion her eldest son
had been injured by a stone thrown into their backyard. The second was
that a neighbour had come round one morning after her husband had
left for work, forced open the door, and started preaching about Islam.
She was frightened that she might be raped, but, fortunately, her driver
returned to the house, and the neighbour left.

In addition to this oral evidence, the representative had also submitted a large bundle of reports and documents, as evidence that Christians were being persecuted in the Sudan. These included a letter from the UNHCR, a report by the US State Department, a report by Human Rights Africa Watch, newspaper reports, and two letters from British academics. The bundle also contained a copy of a circular, which was regularly used in Sudanese appeals, that had been sent by the Sudanese secret service to its agents at ports and airports, instructing them to detain any Christian who had sought asylum in Britain.

The submission of the Presenting Officer was that, although this couple had experienced 'discrimination', they had not suffered persecution under the Convention. He explained the problem of defining persecution in the following terms:

> **"You will know, Maam, there is no standard definition of persecution. The case of Jonah defined it as 'injurious action and oppressive action'. In the case of Ravichandran there is an** *obiter* **remark that it must be 'serious and persistent'. Article 33 of the Convention says 'a serious problem to life and limb'. But I think it is generally accepted that persecution is a serious word [ ]. The Convention uses 'persecution' and never any other word: 'harassment' or 'discrimination'. So, it means something serious and considerably more important than straightforward difficulties with harassment or discrimination."**

He went on to suggest that this couple had experienced 'discrimination', rather than 'persecution', for two reasons. In the first place, when considered in a broader perspective, the 'difficulties' they experienced had to be set against the fact that Mr L had a good job, and his wife was able to attend church every Sunday. In the second place, two recent tribunal decisions had found that there was no persecution of Christians in the Sudan, although there was discrimination.

The first tribunal, chaired by Mr Care, had reviewed all the documentary evidence submitted about the Sudan in a series of decisions by adjudicators which were favourable to appellants. It had concluded that Christians were not being persecuted, and made the following observation about the circular from the secret service:

> **"We have studied the special adjudicators' findings and ... we find the instruction was a forgery, because the British embassy**

– which is independent in the Sudan – would not claim it was a
forgery unless they had good reason to think it to be so."

The second tribunal, chaired by Professor Jackson, agreed with the
UNHCR that people returning to the Sudan with a political background
were at risk, but that not everyone would be interrogated.

In responding to these legal arguments, the representative for the
appellant argued that the ill-treatment the couple had received did amount
to persecution:

> "This is clear persecution and falls in the ambit of paragraph
> 65 of the UNHCR handbook. These are not isolated incidents
> but cumulative and could also have led to detention and physical
> death [ ].
>
> This may not be a case where a threat to life or liberty was
> immediate but the threat was there, and it should not be asked
> of appellants that they have to be tortured before they can claim
> asylum. Mr L knew from his experience with the security forces,
> this is a country unsafe for him to live in. It may well be, given
> what we know of the Sudan, with his history with the security
> forces, we know he would be detained and killed.."

The representative asked the adjudicator to accept the finding of the
UNHCR that the circular was not a forgery, rather than the view of the
Foreign and Commonwealth Office. In any event, this case could be
distinguished from the appeal heard by Professor Jackson because Mr L
was previously known to the security services.

In a 12-page determination, the adjudicator summarised the evidence
and submissions, and came down in favour of the appellants. She noted
that she had read the two cases, and preferred the view in the second[8].
The Tribunal had concluded that "on the evidence, it seems to us that the
Sudanese government is quite capable of arbitrary detention and there is
a risk to any returnee, whether or not an asylum-seeker, of suffering from
persecutory acts". She, therefore, found that the Secretary of State's refusal
of the application "is not in accordance with the Law, the Immigration
Rules and the decided cases".

Appeal 2

This was the appeal of Mr J, a 23-year-old Serb, who had been living in the Republic of Croatia. He arrived in Britain in September 1993, and claimed asylum at the airport. His appeal was heard in April 1996.

Mr J told the court that he had been planning to leave Croatia since 1992 when he received call-up papers to serve in the army. He felt that he would be vulnerable as a Serb, and did not want to fight against members of his family who lived in Serbia. He did not leave until 1993, when he received a further letter from the army, because it was difficult to do so; he had a girlfriend in Croatia, and needed to make proper arrangements. He did not believe it was possible to do 'civilian service' in the Croatian army.

Mr J had also received threats over the telephone from anonymous callers because he was a Serb. He did not report these to the police, because the authorities in Croatia would simply regard this kind of thing as a "quarrel between neighbours". His brother did not have any problems living in Croatia, and had a Croatian wife. However, he had a first name that immediately identified him as being Serbian. This meant that he was always likely to face discrimination in finding work.

The Presenting Officer made the following submission:

> **"Sir, I rely on the Secretary of State's refusal letter. Basically, there are two issues:**
>
> **[First], the problems he would encounter as a Serb in Croatia. He has received threats. I would ask you to consider that these are not as serious as he makes out. He remained in secure accommodation. He had a passport and an identity card. He received threats, yet he regarded matters like his girlfriend as more important [in delaying his departure]. He did not report the threats to the police, and they clearly cannot be linked to the state.**
>
> **He claims that discrimination can occur in employment. I would ask you to note this does not necessarily amount to persecution [ ]. I would also point out that unemployment is a fact of life, and while there may be some discrimination, unemployment remains high for all Croatians [ ].**

I submit that his departure relates more to his wish to evade
military service. He claims that civilian service does not exist.
I would ask you to consider that the evidence referred to in
various documents and determinations before you is that it
does exist [ ].

I do not propose to take you through the determinations before
you. I have noted the determinations supplied by the appellant
– many of which say the opposite – and many general documents
relating to conditions in Croatia.

I would ask you, Sir, to apply the usual standards and dismiss
the appeal."

In her reply, the appellant's representative reviewed a number of decisions
by adjudicators and The Tribunal about conscientious objection. These
suggested that one could claim asylum for a Convention reason provided
that there was a risk of "disproportionately severe punishment" for evading
military service. According to reports by international organisations,
such as Amnesty International, it was only possible to do 'civilian service'
in the Croatian army, and there was a law punishing returnees who had
evaded the draft with a five- to 20-year prison service. Moreover, Mr J
did not benefit from the terms of an amnesty offered to draft-dodgers by
the Croatian government.

After reviewing the case-law about draft evasion, the adjudicator found
that Mr J had not been evading military service. However, he did accept
that any Serb was at risk of being persecuted in Croatia, and so allowed
the appeal:

"While the Croatian government does not condone
discrimination against minorities, in the present turmoil in that
country, bearing in mind the US State Department Reports, I
find that the Croatian government has neither the will, nor the
ability to protect its citizens of minority descent. On this head,
I am satisfied on the totality of the evidence, and having applied
the lower standard of proof, that there is at least a possibility
that the appellant will suffer persecution if he is returned to
Croatia, and that such persecution would be for a Convention
reason. For this reason, the appeal is allowed."

Appeal 3

This was the appeal of a Kurd from Turkey who arrived in Britain in 1995, and claimed asylum at the airport. The appeal took place in December 1996.

The appellant's evidence was that he had been arrested a number of times in Turkey because of his activities in distributing leaflets for TKPMLH, the political wing of a militant Kurdish organisation which had recently been responsible for a number of bombings. Each time he had been given fallaca, a method of torture which involved beating the soles of the feet. He had continued distributing leaflets until he learnt that a friend had been arrested by the police who would be able to identify him as a member of the TKPMLH.

The Secretary of State's letter had refused the application on a number of grounds. These included the fact that the authorities were justified in investigating his activities, because he was a member of an illegal organisation. It was also suggested that, because his parents and three uncles were already in the United Kingdom as political refugees, he had fabricated this story to join his family. It was significant that he only had a "basic understanding" of the TKPMLH, rather than the understanding of "someone who was actually involved".

His representative asked him the following questions on this point:

R: **Can you tell us what the TKPH is?**

W: **They defend TKPMLH actions. They defend the rights of workers, the rights of arrested people, and their aim is to stand by such oppressed people from whom their rights have been taken away.**

R: **And who founded the TKPMLH?**

W: **His name is Ibrahim Kaypakaya.**

R: **Can you spell his second name?**

W: **K A Y P A K A Y A**

R: **And if I said to you which concept of communism do the TKPMLH follow, what would you say?**

W: **There are no different concepts in communism.**

R: **So, what do you mean by that?**

W: **Communism is a world-wide system of labourers and peasants.**

The appellant had received no lasting physical injuries from the fallaca, but gave evidence that he was unable to concentrate and often had bad nightmares. He had a stutter (which was sometimes evident in his answers) and claimed that this had been caused by the torture. His representative had obtained a 12-page medical report from a psychologist who concluded that he was suffering from a form of post-traumatic stress disorder.

In his closing submission, the Presenting Officer suggested that there was no evidence to corroborate his claims of being tortured, since it was just as likely "he had stammered all his life". If the court accepted his story, he had brought the persecution on himself through having continued to sell newspapers. This was a case of prosecution, rather than persecution, since the TKPMLH was an illegal organisation.

His representative argued that he was selling newspapers for a legitimate political party. Reports about the political circumstances also provided sufficient corroboration of his story, and so, on the test of reasonable likelihood, the adjudicator should allow the appeal.

Appeal 4

This was the appeal of Mr W, a 56-year-old Tamil from Sri Lanka, who had arrived in Britain in 1995, and claimed asylum at the airport. The hearing took place in March 1997.

The appellant's evidence was that he had been approached by the Tamil Tigers and asked for help, but had refused. He had then been arrested on three occasions by the Sri Lankan authorities, and had been in hiding for a year before leaving the country. He had spent some time in Columbo, but had also experienced trouble with the police there.

In her submission, the Presenting Officer noted that there was a discrepancy between his evidence at the hearing, and his account in the interview, about the number of times he had been arrested, and it seemed improbable that he had remained in hiding a year without coming to the attention of the authorities. She also did not believe that the army let him go after two hours when he was first detained, just because he begged to be released:

H: **It seems he was released the first time, simply because he pleaded. Sir, that's simply not credible.**

A: **Why not?**

H: **It's certainly not to me, Sir. If armed forces, doing their jobs, arrest you because you're part of a terrorist group, pleading with them would not be enough.**

The main point made by the representative for the appellant was that, irrespective of whether or not the appellant's account was found to be credible, there had been a serious terrorist incident the previous week in which 200 people had died. This indicated that there was still a state of disorder in Sri Lanka, and no one should be returned to the country.

Before reserving his determination, the adjudicator asked the Presenting Officer to ascertain from the Home Office if their policy of returning appellants to Sri Lanka had changed in view of the latest events. Although the adjudicator found against Mr W, he also noted that he would not be returned to Sri Lanka while the capital Columbo was considered unsafe.

Appeal 5

This was the appeal of a woman from Zaïre who had arrived in Britain in 1989, and claimed asylum when she was found working as an illegal immigrant in 1996. The appeal took place in November 1997.

She told the court that she was claiming asylum because she was a member of the IBM, a political party opposed to president Mbutu. She had represented 32 class-mates as a student leader for this party. She had also attended a violent demonstration in Kinshassa, and had been arrested and put in prison for 10 months. She had not been beaten, but had once been slapped by a solider for biting him. She had been released by her uncle who was in the army. Since leaving Zaïre, she had received a letter from her sister saying that her uncle and younger brother had been killed.

The Presenting Officer wanted to know how she knew that her uncle and brother had been killed:

H: When was your brother killed?

W: My uncle and younger brother were arrested and killed. Unlike in this country where everyone is responsible and accountable for his doings, in my country you can be arrested for what your relatives have done. Because of that they were arrested and killed [ ].

H: There is no mention in the letters that were handed in of your uncle being killed.

W: In the letters, it was mentioned that several people died because of me, and I am certain it was my uncle and younger brother.

H: I will actually state what it says here. It says some of your friends were arrested and killed. Your uncle was arrested and put in prison. How do you interpret that to mean your uncle had been killed?

W: That is what you are saying: that my uncle was arrested and put in prison. For me, my uncle was [ ] and killed because he was arrested. No one has had his news. Furthermore, I was born in Kinshassa, and know how things are.

In his closing submission, the Presenting Officer noted that the letter from her sister must have been 'self-serving', since a letter she had received a month previously did not mention the fact that her brother had been killed. He suggested that:

"... the only reason why she asked someone in Zaïre to send letters is because she knows her claim is fraudulent, and she has to bolster it in some way. There is no reason to embellish or put in fraudulent documents if her claim is true."

Appeal 6

This was the appeal of Mr T, a 21-year-old man from the Ivory Coast. He arrived in the United Kingdom in January 1994 and claimed asylum a month later. His appeal was heard in November 1997.

Mr T told the court that he had taken part in a demonstration outside his school, when it was announced that it would be closed by the government. He and three friends had been charged with criminal damage to documents and computers. He had then gone into hiding, and a friend of his mother who was a captain in the army had arranged his escape from the Ivory Coast. The documents he gave to the immigration officers at the airport suggested that he had come to England to study, and he had been given a visa to stay in the country for six months. He was aware there had been an amnesty in the Ivory Coast in 1992, but felt that if he returned he might be sentenced to 20 years in prison. His brother had said that he would write when it was safe for him to return, but he had not heard from him since 1994. He was a member of a political party called the FPI, but had not mentioned this when he was interviewed.

The adjudicator questioned this appellant at length about how he had left the Ivory Coast. His evidence had been that the captain had 'dealt with officials', and had given him his passport when he boarded the plane. He had kept the ticket while they were at the airport. The adjudicator wanted to know how the hostess had been able to direct him to his seat without a boarding card:

A: **How did you know which seat to sit on in the aircraft?**

W: **When I boarded the plane, I showed the ticket to the flight attendant, and she seated me.**

A: **That's not true, is it?**

W: **Why?**

A: **You don't have seat numbers on tickets. You can't board airports by going through passport control without your ticket with you. It can't be done.**

W: **The airline ticket was given to me before I got to the airport.**

A: **Yes, but the captain would have had to have it to check you in. Without your ticket it can't be done.**

In his determination, the adjudicator refused the appeal on three grounds. In the first place, he felt that Mr T's account lacked 'credibility' in a number of areas. He was particularly suspicious about the way he had left the Ivory Coast, and arrived in Britain:

> **"I believe that he came to the United Kingdom to be a student. He did not come because he was fleeing for his life or at risk in respect of his liberty. I believe that when he arrived, he indicated his intentions at the time to the Immigration Officer, and the application for asylum was an afterthought."**

He also found it "difficult to believe" that the appellant had been unable to supply recent information about what had happened to his friends on the demonstration:

> **"I do not find very satisfactory the evidence of the appellant that his brother ... knows his address and, if anything had happened, would have written to him. The appellant, in bringing his appeal, produces the evidence which he does produce, and it is up to him to produce any other evidence which is available. In the absence of anything further from his brother, with whom he is in touch, I am bound to remark that the evidence with regard to the continued detention of the appellant's friends is from early 1994, and it is remarkable that the evidence should not be available as to the situation since then."**

In the second place, even if the appellant had been charged with criminal damage, he feared 'prosecution' rather than 'persecution'. The government of the Ivory Coast were entitled to pass a law discouraging students from engaging in violence and damage to property. Finally, the amnesty announced by the government in 1992 covered the offences of the appellant, so there was no reason to fear being returned to the Ivory Coast.

Some features of decision making in asylum appeals

Although they only provide a taste of the evidence presented in these hearings, these case studies make it possible to appreciate how three of the four general grounds of refusal I listed earlier in the chapter, became relevant in particular appeals. These were that there was no Convention reason, subjective fear or objective circumtances to justify the claim.

Deciding if there is a Convention reason

The first task of the adjudicator, in assessing any appeal, is to determine whether or not there is a Convention reason to claim asylum. In Appeal 1, the main issue the adjudicator had to decide was whether the ill-treatment was of sufficient magnitude and duration to qualify as persecution. Perhaps inevitably, the definitions supplied in the UNHCR handbook, and in leading cases such as *Jonah*, are extremely vague, which would have made it possible for this couple to have appealed to a higher court, if the adjudicator had refused the appeal.

In Appeals 3 and 6, the Home Office argued that the appellants were fleeing from prosecution, rather than persecution. The Turkish appellant had been involved in an illegal organisation; and the student from the Ivory Coast had committed a criminal offence. In other appeals, adjudicators sometimes had to refuse people who clearly deserved help, but did not qualify for refugee status under the Convention. They were entitled to make recommendations to the Home Office to grant Exceptional Leave to Remain, but these were only rarely followed. One adjudicator told me about an appeal involving a Kenyan woman:

> **"There was this person in an area where two lots of soldiers clashed, and she was raped and then kept as the mistress of a soldier, and I believed her, and she got out of the country. She was not persecuted for a Convention reason, but was in the wrong place at the wrong time. I felt she needed sympathetic treatment. Therefore, I made a recommendation .... This one wasn't followed."**

In many appeals, however, there was a Convention reason, and the purpose of the hearing was to establish if the fear of persecution was well-founded.

Deciding if there is a subjective fear

A large number of asylum appeals are dismissed on the grounds that the appellant is found to lack 'credibility'. Here, it is worth identifying three institutional perspectives on the oral evidence presented by appellants about their experience of persecution.

Presenting Officers

The main task of Home Office Presenting Officers is to persuade the adjudicator that the appellant has exaggerated the ill-treatment which they have experienced, or even made up the whole story in order to make an asylum claim in Britain. There are a number of ways in which this is done during hearings, depending on the nature of the evidence.

In many appeals, there are discrepancies between the initial interview, and the account presented to the court. In Appeal 3, for example, the appellant had not been able to tell the Home Office the name of the founder of the TKPMLH in his interview, although he did so during the hearing. In Appeal 4, the appellant said that he had been arrested twice by the Sri Lankan army in his interview, but remembered a further arrest by the time of the hearing. In Appeal 6, the appellant had told the interviewers that he did not belong to a political party, which was necessary in order for him to claim asylum in these circumstances under the Convention. In the hearing, however, he told the court that he was a member of the FPI, but that he had left his membership card in the Ivory Coast.

A second way in which Presenting Officers try to undermine the credibility of appellants is by identifying implausible events, lacunae, or internal contradictions. In Appeal 4, it was suggested that the fact an appellant had been quickly released from custody as a suspected terrorist was implausible, which threw doubt upon the rest of his testimony. In Appeal 5, it was suggested that none of the appellant's evidence should be believed since she had tried to give the court the false impression that her uncle had died as a result of helping her leave Zaïre. Finally, in Appeal 6, two contradictions were identified. The first was that the appellant had arrived in England wishing to seek asylum, but had not done so at the airport. The second was that he had given an account of how he left the Ivory Coast which seemed implausible, in view of how international airlines usually operate.

Representatives

Although it was possible for any case to be undermined in this way, representatives could also use similar techniques to persuade adjudicators that the appellant was a credible witness. Gaps or problems in the account given in the initial interview could, for example, often be explained by the fact that the appellant was disoriented by the journey, still suffering from trauma as a result of being tortured, or afraid of British officials. Failure to remember the exact details of events from several years ago (including names and dates) was understandable 'given the circumstances', and should not mean that every aspect of the appellant's evidence should be disbelieved.

In the appeals in this sample, representatives had no difficulty in finding counter-arguments about pieces of evidence in their closing submissions. In Appeal 3, it was suggested that there was nothing amiss about the appellant's answers about communism, since someone from a rural background should not be expected to know the finer points of party ideology. In Appeals 4 and 5, it was submitted that the points made by the Home Office did not affect the overall credibility of the appellant, and that some degree of 'embellishment' was understandable, given the circumstances. In Appeal 6, it was suggested that the appellant did not claim asylum at the airport because he was following instructions from the captain. The fact that he had been able to travel on the plane to England without a boarding card may simply have been because the stewardess directed him to an empty seat.

Representatives did not always believe the clients they represented in court. One described his doubts about a particular appellant in the following terms:

> "He waited three months before claiming asylum in the last month his visa was up, so it's not consistent with someone fearing persecution ... if he had a fear of persecution he should do it at the airport ... rather than working for three months, and, finding you can't do anything else, then claim. So his whole story is just ... I mean, I've seen him talking and I don't believe him. It may look OK on paper, but it will become apparent at the hearing, he just doesn't supply enough detail about the incidents when he's been arrested."

This appellant's claim was based on the fact he had been arrested three times, and on one of these occasions a friend had been thrown off a balcony by the security forces. There were, however, a number of things about his account the court would not believe, which cumulatively made it a weak case:

> "The reason why they won't believe him – well, I certainly have my doubts – is that I can't picture this person standing in

a hall with, you know, hundreds of other people, that's what he said to me. Suddenly, these police officers come bursting in. Although I can believe that, why would they want to pick on him, why didn't they take the priest away, or someone else who was organising it? ... I can see why someone would believe that, but I would want to know why they would identify him.

He's taken away. He's taken to the police station, is beaten up or whatever. He's taken to the court the next day, and he says to me the lawyer there did nothing, but they released him anyway. Fine. Then he says he went back to his room. He was sitting in his room, and the police arrested him and his two friends again. The same sort of thing happened – he was beaten up and released.

The third time ... there must have been about a thousand people on the student campus, and again the police came in the middle of this crowd, and managed to somehow – I find it difficult to believe that the policeman came up to him and said 'You're all under arrest' in plain clothes, and then they managed to get away. Because if they're going to get that far, close to them, these three people, they're going to be nabbed, they're not going to have the chance to run away. And the thing is, I can't believe why there was so much attention on them. If they wanted them so much, they would have taken them before at the second arrest. And then his friend gets thrown out of a balcony. OK, and if you want to believe that he's still alive after that, he goes to the hospital to talk to his friend, decides he wants to leave the country, and then just disappears. He stays in the country for another nine months, makes no attempt to leave, but when he does leave he goes to the British embassy, and gets a visa to come over here ... I mean there's just too many...."

In this case, there were too many gaps and discrepancies in the appellant's evidence, so the representative knew that it would be difficult to persuade the adjudicator to accept his account at the hearing.

Adjudicators

The adjudicators in these appeals had to decide whether or not they believed the appellant through employing the test of 'reasonable likelihood'. In Appeal 1, the adjudicator found in her determination that the Sudanese couple were totally credible as witnesses. In Appeals 2, 3 and 4, the adjudicators believed much of the account presented to them. In Appeals 5 and 6, the adjudicators found the account of the appellant to be completely lacking in credibility.

After a while, adjudicators knew more-or-less what to expect from appellants seeking asylum from different countries. Some decisions were easy to make, if it was recognised that there were no objective circumstances in that country to support an appeal. So, for example, the adjudicator hearing the Ivory Coast appeal, already knew that it was likely to fail before hearing the evidence. Other appeals came from countries where it was recognised that persecution was taking place. It was evident that Presenting Officers and representatives spent more time preparing for these hearings, and adjudicators told me that they often found it hard reaching a decision.

To give an indication about how adjudicators viewed the task of assessing credibility, here are some comments about two of the appeals in my sample:

a) Appeal 3 (Turkish appellant)

> "The Kurds in Turkey are definitely second class citizens. They are not necessarily persecuted, but they are not allowed to speak their own language in schools or in public. Generally speaking, they are looked on as terrorists, and a lot of them are in the PKK, or are supporters because of their ambition to have their own state. They live in a region within Turkey, Iraq and Iran, and they have suffered in those three countries, and even among the Kurds there are internal conflicts. So, you get a lot of Kurdish cases.

> They are very difficult cases. Very often you will find yourself having some sympathy. Then you will find they are not considered to be persecuted *per se*, although it's close. They tend to be taken in and beaten on the soles of their feet (it's called fallaca), and they tend to exaggerate. There are never any documents they can produce but an abundance of background information.

It all comes down to credibility. They all want to come to the UK. The question is if they are just telling a pack of lies."

b) Appeal 5 (Zaïrian appellant)

"I think, evidentially, my first reaction was [looks through his notes made during the hearing] I had doubts about whether she was really detained as she said ... but on the other hand, you see, my initial impression of her was not really terribly impressive, and not very good at all. But that could have been largely due to the way her case was presented, you see, it was such a mess, her examination-in-chief. In some parts of her evidence, she did exaggerate, but once she got cracking she didn't sort of say, 'Oh, I was beaten up regularly by soldiers'. There was one occasion when she sort of got slapped, when she bit a soldier when she resisted being put in a cell. And that seems to be quite likely, but I am always a bit suspicious of people who get out of prison through a relative....

The difficulty is the letters. What she was saying about the uncle clearly isn't born out by these letters.... What we've got to decide on the basis of a reasonable degree of likelihood is what exactly has happened. Was that lady detained, was she released when she says she was.... And once you've got that established, what you might find is that someone might have a good claim, but has sought to bolster it with additional lurid details. If these lurid details are untrue, how much of the whole thing does that undermine.... I find [this appeal] quite difficult, and will have to read it through again to see where we end up."

In deciding these appeals, the problem for adjudicators was that the only evidence they had was the account given by the appellant. In the Turkish appeal, for example, there was a 12-page medical report from a firm of psychologists who specialised in providing evidence in asylum appeals. According to the adjudicator, the report simply reproduced the appellant's evidence in the hearing, although there was a standard two pages of 'psychological jargon' about post-traumatic stress disorder. He usually placed more weight on reports from consultants, or official organisations like the Medical Foundation for Victims of Torture.

Most adjudicators were open about the fact that it was possible to make a mistake on credibility (one told me, "We've all done it"), but they felt the job was made easier by the fact that it was always possible to appeal. One expressed this in the following terms:

> "The job we do is not fun, it's not entertaining, it's not dealing with entertaining things. Some of the things we have to listen to.... If you took them home at night, and thought about them, you could drive yourself mad. The only way I can cope is to enjoy the intellectual exercise in using the procedural rules, the law and so on, and, as far as the cases are concerned, to call the shots the way I see them. There's also the reassurance if I make a mistake, there always are other people far better qualified to sort it out."

Deciding if there is an objective risk of persecution

Even if an appellant was believed, the adjudicator had to decide if there was an objective risk that the appellant would be persecuted for a Convention reason if returned to their country of nationality. To prove this, the appellant's representative submitted a large bundle of documents, including newspaper articles, and reports from different international organisations or academic experts. Some appellants also called witnesses to give background information about the current political situation in their own country. Many of these were themselves asylum-seekers, or had recently obtained refugee status.

Experienced adjudicators tended to have their own views about the evidential value of different reports. One adjudicator told me that the country reports produced by the Home Office often presented a rosy view of political problems in particular countries. However, it was necessary to be discriminating in reading other reports:

> "Amnesty reports I find less helpful than most others. They tend to be very campaigning in style which I don't find helpful, and it's quite instructive to read what Amnesty says about the UK and then set it in context.... If you read what they say about the UK, it's not a place you'd want to go to.
>
> [The US State Department Reports] are quite helpful, but depending on which country's involved you have to be a little

careful because they're written from the perspective of the US
government so they might be slanted also.... For instance,
reading their report on Columbia or South American countries
where they tend to get people coming in, I would regard the
US State Department Report with more circumspection that I
might regard their report on India."

In general, adjudicators tended to place most weight on reports by the
US State Department and United Nations High Commissioner for
Refugees, and less weight on letters supplied by academic 'experts'.

Because adjudicators were required to make a finding of fact about
conditions in a particular country, in the same way as would a jury, they
were not expected to be consistent in the way they interpreted documentary
evidence. In Appeal 1, for example, another adjudicator might have reached
a different conclusion about the risks facing Coptic Christians who returned
to the Sudan. In Appeal 2, it would have been possible to have come to a
different view about the existence of 'civilian service' in the Croatian
army, or what would happen to deserters (although this assessment was
not, in the end, significant in determining the outcome of this appeal).

However, because cases could be appealed, a general consensus tended
to develop among decision makers at adjudicator level and in The Tribunal,
over the course of time, about conditions in particular countries. It was
generally agreed, for example, that you had a good chance of being
recognised as a refugee if you were a Coptic Christian from the Sudan, a
Serb from Croatia, or a Kurd from Turkey, since there was strong objective
evidence to suggest that persecution of these groups was taking place.
On the other hand, it was extremely hard for anyone from India to win
an appeal. This was because, although there were political conflicts in
areas like the Punjab which might create refugees, most appellants could
reasonably be expected to move to another area of the country where
they would be safe.

There were, however, exceptions when a consensus about conditions
in a particular country failed to emerge. One adjudicator told me that
there was not much consistency in deciding appeals from Sri Lanka:

"[This] causes tremendous problems because adjudicators tend
to take different positions on whether Tamils are safe in
government controlled areas of Columbo. Some really take the
view that all Tamils are safe, full stop, and that the government
are doing it not as persecution under the Convention but to

> maintain security.... You can say that all the facts are infinitely different and that every Tamil will have been doing a lot of different things, but part of the problem is that most Tamils who are up in the north will have been forced to cooperate with the LTT if they were there. They had no alternative. The argument is that, under those circumstances, inevitably, they are going to be looked at very carefully by the Sri Lankan authorities in Columbo in a situation where there are terrorist outrages, and where the Tamil Tigers do use the fact there are refugees going down to infiltrate their own terrorists into Columbo. It's a very difficult assessment to have to make."

Opinion was sharply divided during my fieldwork about whether or not Columbo, the capital of Sri Lanka, could be regarded as a safe area. A series of tribunal decisions favoured the Home Office, but some adjudicators still adopted a different view of the evidence. Renewed violence in Sri Lanka caused opinion to shift towards the appellant in the autumn of 1996.

Is there a 'culture of refusal' in deciding asylum appeals?

In presenting this account of some features of decision making in six cases, I have not yet addressed the issue raised by critics of the court-system that adjudicators dismiss too many asylum appeals. In a quantitative study based on an analysis of 722 determinations, Alison Harvey (1996) notes that it is difficult to assess how decisions are made on credibility, although it is possible to identify inconsistencies in the way adjudicators assess objective circumstances. She suggests that there is a need for more research, based on observation of hearings, and the analysis of determinations, which can be used in training adjudicators and other practitioners.

The case studies I have discussed provide some degree of insight into how decisions were made in a few appeals. However, it would clearly be impossible to re-determine any one of these appeals, after the event, without having access to all the evidence (including the various reports about 'objective circumstances') in the same way as the adjudicator in an actual hearing; and, in any case, one can hardly generalise from how decisions were made in six cases to the thousands of appeals that are heard each year in the courts.

On the other hand, the qualitative sociologist can contribute to this debate by clarifying what seems to be at issue between different institutional perspectives in the courts. The following points are made in this spirit:

1. The majority of asylum appeals are refused on the grounds of credibility, rather than, for example, because there is no Convention reason for making the claim (Harvey, 1996). In most of these, the only evidence, other than reports about 'objective circumstances' in different countries, is the account given by the appellant.

2. All practitioners, including appellants' representatives, recognise that there are many 'evidentially weak' cases in the courts. These are often described in moral terms as 'bogus' claims. A recurrent finding in sociological studies of public service organisations is that practitioners become 'case-hardened', through having to process large numbers of claims (Lipsky, 1980), and quickly learn to distinguish between 'deserving' and 'undeserving' clients. Becker et al (1961), for example, note that medical students described people with certain kinds of illnesses as 'crocks', who would not assist them in learning about medicine. Adjudicators, Presenting Officers and representatives have a similar attitude towards appellants with 'weak' claims: they take up organisational resources, and limit the time practitioners can spend on more interesting and deserving cases.

3. Many of these 'weak' claims are from appellants in countries where there is little objective risk of persecution. A good example is India, which in Harvey's sample, made up roughly 17% of appeals being heard in the courts in 1995, in which no appellant was successful in winning an appeal. By contrast, there were no successful appeals from the Ivory Coast (Appeal 6 in my sample) but they made up only 0.9% of appeals[9].

4. However, a large proportion of appeals are still refused in countries where it is agreed that persecution is taking place. According to Harvey, the recognition rates for the countries in the first five appeals in my sample were the following in 1995: Sudan (0.9% appeals) – 28.5% allowed; Croatia (0.6% appeals) – 40% allowed; Turkey (5.4% appeals) – 40% allowed; Sri Lanka (5.6%) – 15% allowed; Zaïre (1.1%) – 12.5% allowed.

5. Different occupational groups in the courts have different views on the issue of refusals, which are based on their own experience of

representing parties, or deciding cases, often over a period of years. Presenting Officers are generally cynical about the claims made by asylum-seekers, and believe, with some conviction, that adjudicators allow too many appeals. Representatives working for the IAS and Refugee Legal Centre, on the other hand, believe that adjudicators are far too ready to dismiss the evidence presented in hearings[10]. On the other hand, adjudicators themselves believe that, even by applying the low standard of proof, they are still only able to allow a small number of appeals.

6. Defenders of the status quo would want to argue that anyone would refuse a similar percentage of appeals. Critics, on the other hand, have suggested that new adjudicators are inevitably influenced by the 'culture of refusal' that already exists, and by the negative image of asylum-seekers in the media. From this perspective, the only way to get fairer decisions would either mean re-educating practitioners, or setting up a new organisation to make decisions[11]. There have, as yet, been no detailed proposals on how to change the way adjudicators make decisions.

Notes

[1] Exceptional Leave to Remain is granted for one year, and can then be extended for two futher periods of three years. Settlement is usually granted after seven years.

[2] All determinations made by adjudicators are sent to this office under the 1993 Asylum and Immigration Act. However, owing to a shortage of staff and resources, very few of these are actually read, and UNHCR officials only make representations to the Home Office about general categories of appeals.

[3] Asylum applications in Germany rose from 73,800 in 1985 to 438,200 in 1992; and in America from under 5,000 in 1979 to over 140,000 in 1994. This can be compared with a rise in Britain from 4,400 in 1985 to 44,800 in 1991 (Mortimer, 1996).

[4] Full details of the different groups claiming asylum, and success rates, can be found in the annual Asylum Statistics published by the Home Office. There has been some variation in the nationalities claiming asylum, which partly reflects political events around the world. The figures for 1997 show an increase in the

percentage of applications from Europe to 28% out of 32,500 applicants, and a decrease in the percentage from Africa and Asia to 56%. The respective figures in 1995 were 16% and 75%.

[5] See *R v Secretary of State for the Home Department ex parte Sivakumaran* [1988] ImmAR 147 [HL], and [1987] 3 WLR 1047 [CA].

[6] This construction of the 'reasonable likelihood' test was widely used by adjudicators, until it was criticised by Professor Jackson in The Tribunal. He argued that it was meaningless to quantify the burden of proof in this way, and threatened to remit any appeal for a re-hearing, in which a determination had contained the phrase '10% chance of persecution'.

[7] The adjudicators hearing these appeals told me that they had not reached a decision during the hearing, and would have to consider the evidence carefully before writing their determinations.

[8] Shortly after this hearing, the Court of Appeal resolved the uncertainty created by these conflicting tribunal decisions by ruling that it was unsafe for Christians to return to the Sudan. The references for these cases are: *Drrias* (14060) IAT; *Mohammed Ali* (1412) IAT; and *Atif Ali Drrias v Secretary of State for the Home Department* [1997] ImmAR 346 [CA].

[9] For an account of one hearing, in which the appellant admitted to being an economic migrant, see Travers (1996).

[10] Both groups accepted that there were well known exceptions who did refuse or allow most appeals. Refusal rates for individual adjudicators are unknown, and it would be interesting to see if there are anomalous clusters within the overall high refusal rate, resulting from 'liberal' or 'hard' adjudicators. Such a finding would not be especially surprising. See, for example, Hood's (1992) study of racial bias in sentencing, which suggests, in delicate terms, that variations can be accounted for by the prejudices of particular judges.

[11] This is also a common argument used by critics of the police and defence lawyers. See Travers (1997a).

SIX

The courts as an
administrative problem

Although many academic studies have been concerned with the interaction of lawyers, witnesses and judges in the courtroom, there have been few attempts to examine the routine administrative work which takes place behind-the-scenes in maintaining any court-system[1]. In this chapter, I want to examine the immigration courts mainly from the perspective of civil servants in the Home Office and Lord Chancellor's Department during the period 1996-97, and look at the effect of changes made during this period on other organisations in the court-system. I will also be discussing the 1999 Immigration and Asylum Bill, which will have received its third reading in Parliament by the time this book is published.

I will begin by providing a general introduction to the perspective of the civil service in this area of government policy. I will then provide an account of some of the administrative work involved in making the 1996 Asylum and Immigration Act, and the new procedural rules that came into effect in September of that year. I will also examine the effect of these, and other changes that were taking place, on the work of managers and practitioners in the Immigration Advisory Service (IAS), a unit of Home Office Presenting Officers, and the Immigration Appellate Authority. I will then discuss developments after 1997, including the changes that will result from the 1999 Act, and conclude by considering the practical alternatives open to policy makers in managing the immigration courts.

The civil service perspective

When the immigration courts were set up by the 1969 Immigration (Appeals) Act, they were initially made the responsibility of the Immigration and Nationality Department in the Home Office. It has the task of making and implementing British policy on immigration and asylum, under the direction of ministers appointed through the political process.

During the 1970s, the Home Office was responsible for all aspects of the appeals process, as well as the initial work of making decisions on applications. It was directly responsible for training and managing the Presenting Officers who represented the government at appeals hearings. It also funded, and exercised ultimate administrative authority over both the United Kingdom Immigration Advisory Service (UKIAS), which provided free advice and assistance to appellants, and the Immigration Appellate Authority which ran the courts.

In 1987, responsibility for the courts was transferred to the Lord Chancellor's Department. However, in terms of accountability to Parliament, and responsibility for making policy, the Home Office remains what civil servants call the 'lead department' in relation to the immigration courts. The 1993 and 1996 Asylum and Immigration Acts, which set up, and then modified, a right of appeal for asylum-seekers, were devised by policy teams in the Immigration and Nationality Department, and introduced into parliament by Home Office ministers. The Lord Chancellor's Department has only a service role in providing the buildings and judicial personnel used in the appeals process, and in making the procedural rules which govern business in the courts.

Most research on the civil service has been undertaken by journalists (for example, Hennessy, 1989) or political scientists, and it tends to concentrate on the relationship between civil servants and ministers in making government policy. There is very little discussion in this literature of the mundane, day-to-day administrative work involved in managing public services. In this respect, government departments can be viewed in much the same terms as other large organisations in the public or private sector. The work of administering the immigration courts involves recruiting personnel, managing budgets, setting targets, and accounting to Parliament and the public in annual reports[2].

One of the civil servants I interviewed in the Lord Chancellor's Department made a distinction between different areas of departmental business:

> "Some things are driven by a minister's ideological or political needs or wishes. Some things are driven by unpleasant reality. It wasn't on anybody's agenda that suddenly there should be a tremendous increase in asylum cases, but suddenly it becomes something that has to be dealt with. The way in which they deal with it [depends on] what the real options are, and what the inclinations of the ministers concerned are.

> Some things are driven by the departments themselves. There is always a massive amount of ongoing business. Generally speaking, it's more the kind of day-to-day things that are just sort of unavoidable background noise. You know, the president of the IAT retires, as he does next year. He has to be replaced by someone. That's the Lord Chancellor's job, and not someone's policy agenda. It's just a fact of life. That person's got to go, and somebody's got to replace him. That work just has to go on. Unless you are prepared to say to ministers, 'We want this to cease to be a background issue. Here's a policy alternative – you abolish The Tribunal!"

According to this view of the civil service, more senior civil servants are only consulted about problems that cannot be dealt with at a lower level:

> "There is a considerable amount of delegated authority as you go down the managerial chain. In my area, I learn those decisions that I can take, and those decisions that I can take subject to getting a bit of advice from my gaffer. Then there are those decisions on which I advise my gaffer what decisions he can take, and those decisions that I don't touch with a bargepole, and hand straight over to my boss."

Another civil servant told me that ministers were usually only consulted when unexpected and difficult problems arose: "no one bombards ministers with paper unless they have to, and often because it's a decision that only ministers can take".

According to these informants, legislation was not dictated by ministers as part of some political agenda, but used by civil servants, in collaboration with ministers, to address a set of ongoing administrative problems. Because old problems were never completely resolved, and new ones constantly emerging, there was always a need for legislation on almost any area of government policy. As one interviewee put it:

> "Policy making is a rolling process. As soon as one Bill finishes, there will be some people thinking 'What are we going to do next? Are we going to do legislation on this point or that point? These are the growing areas. Do we need to legislate for them?'. The policy-making divisions are always asking themselves that question, and they are always thinking some

> way ahead. 'Is a legislative solution the right thing to have?
> When could we [find space in the government's programme]?
> When's the election going to be?'. And all those kinds of issues.
> And what tends to happen is that priorities change as problems
> get bigger or smaller."

Although civil servants were always planning ahead, it was usually only possible to obtain a place in the government's legislative programme for something recognised as a big current problem. Legislation designed to pre-empt a possible problem in three year's time was not normally a feature of government.

The problem of a backlog

The whole immigration appeals system increasingly came to be viewed as an administrative problem by the civil service from the late 1980s, because of the sudden and unexpected increase in applications for asylum.

This immediately created a number of political and administrative problems. To begin with, before 1993, there was no right of appeal in British law for anyone who claimed asylum at ports or airports, and the existing system could not cope with the increased number of in-country applicants. The Home Office also became aware of abuses by asylum-seekers who made multiple applications, which enabled them to obtain certificates that could be used to obtain additional social security payments. The 1993 Asylum and Immigration Act was a response to these two problems. It established a right of appeal for all asylum applicants (while at the same time removing an existing right of appeal by visitors who were refused entry to the United Kingdom). It also gave immigration officials the power to finger-print asylum-seekers, and so prevent multiple applications[3].

According to the civil servants I interviewed, the new system had some initial success in keeping up with applications. However, the provisions made by both the Home Office and the Lord Chancellor's Department quickly proved to be inadequate:

> "The '93 Act ... was supposed to do the business in terms of
> asylum and did, at first, do the business in terms of reducing
> the decision times on applications. They were brought down to
> almost three months. The aim was to decide an asylum
> application in three months, and I think they almost did that

> **[ie, the previous team]. But just as they got there, the number
> of applications for asylum doubled over two years. So, in 1991
> they had 22,000 asylum applications. In 1995 they had 44,000.
> So, in those two years, it doubled and the system that the '93
> Act was designed for was not those numbers, but to cope with
> the existing intake."**

The unexpected rise in applications after 1993 resulted in a growing
backlog at all stages of the appeals process. The courts could not hear all
the appeals sent to them by the Home Office in any given year, and the
Home Office were also unable to keep up with new applications. There
were long delays in reaching an initial decision, and in listing appeals.
The result is that some asylum-seekers who submitted an application
before 1993 had to wait several years for an initial decision or appeal
hearing[4].

The fact that there were delays in the appeals process was not, in itself,
a problem for government departments. There had, for example, been
considerable delays in processing the applications of people seeking entry
under the primary purpose rule, and other sections of the immigration
rules in the 1980s, without this resulting in initiatives to improve the
speed and efficiency of the Home Office or the courts (Pannick et al,
1993). This backlog was, however, larger and growing year by year. It
also had considerable financial implications in that asylum-seekers were
entitled to claim social security and other benefits. Whatever the views
of the Home Office, ministers are likely to have come under pressure
from the Department of Social Security, and the Treasury, following the
1993 Act, to reduce the annual public expenditure on asylum-seekers.

The making of the 1996 Asylum and Immigration Act

During 1996, when I was doing most of my fieldwork, the piece of
government legislation that was most in the news, and attracted most
criticism from the opposition, was the Asylum and Immigration Bill which
became law in September, after a difficult passage through Parliament. In
the next chapter, I will be looking at some of the political debate that
took place in Parliament about this issue. Here, however, I am interested
in the civil service perspective on the 1996 Act: on the administrative
purposes of this piece of legislation, and how it formed part of ongoing
'business' in a number of government departments. I will begin by
discussing the immediate context in a number of other initiatives being

pursued by the Home Office to reduce the backlog after 1993. I will then attempt to give some sense of the practical difficulties experienced by civil servants in obtaining time in the government's legislative programme, and in securing the passage of the Act through Parliament. I will then consider some other measures contained in the Act, and consider the extent to which it was successful in addressing the problem of the backlog.

The context of the Act

The Home Office view of policy on asylum after 1993 was premised on the assumption (strongly disputed by pressure groups representing refugees) that the majority of people who sought asylum were either 'economic migrants' or 'benefits tourists'. In the view of one interviewee, the rise in numbers of asylum-seekers, therefore, left the government with three options:

> "It can do nothing. It can throw more resources at it, and carry on the same procedures. Or it can look at a way in which it can maximise its use of existing resources. And if that doesn't work, it can take steps to change the law to stop the abuse. So that's the sort of considerations that you are always going to consider."

In the two years prior to the introduction of the Bill in 1995, the Home Office took three measures that were intended to address the problem of the backlog. These were: the investment of new resources through a Spend-to-Save initiative; the removal of social security benefits from some asylum-seekers (both measures that were taken in conjunction with the Department of Social Security); and the introduction of a new system, known as the Short-Procedure, for making the initial decision on applications.

The Spend-to-Save initiative

One way to have enabled the appeals system to cope with an increased number of appellants after 1994 would have been to spend more money on the courts. This was politically impossible given the tough constraints on spending experienced by all government departments since the early 1980s. However, a cross-departmental Spend-to-Save initiative did result in £200 million being transferred from the Department of Social Security to the Home Office and Lord Chancellor's Department over a three-year period from 1994[5].

The thinking behind Spend-to-Save was that the Social Security budget could be reduced over a period of years, through investing money in the appeals process. The civil servants I interviewed in the Lord Chancellor's Department described how the initiative emerged through the 'standard Whitehall network' in the following terms:

A1: **It started, I think, in the DSS and the Treasury as one of a whole range of options of things that somebody could spend money on to effect a saving in the Social Security budget, and there are also all kinds of fraud initiatives. I don't know what the process was that brought in the Home Office, and ultimately the Lord Chancellor's Department. I think the DSS started it.**

A2: **It is sometimes difficult to say that anybody started it, this kind of initiative. It begins as a germ in somebody's mind, and they talk to somebody else over the phone, bring a few people in, and gradually the nature of the idea changes when you get more people involved, and then, almost without realising it, you get an initiative on your hands.**

A1: **It can change quite a lot. The original sponsor can end up with a package he didn't want at all, that was not what he originally wanted [laughs].**

The Department of Social Security may ultimately have felt that they did not obtain a good deal from this Spend-to-Save initiative, since social security benefits were withdrawn from a large number of asylum-seekers, in any event, following a separate policy decision by ministers in 1996. However, the Spend-to-Save money did allow the court-system to expand considerably in an attempt to reduce the backlog. It allowed the Immigration Appellate Authority to open new hearing centres and employ more adjudicators, the Home Office to recruit more Presenting Officers, and the IAS and Refugee Legal Centre to take on new representatives while I was doing my fieldwork.

The removal of benefits from some asylum-seekers

As well as investing money in the appeals system, the government also took the more controversial measure of using its powers under secondary legislation to withdraw benefits from asylum-seekers who did not immediately claim asylum on their arrival in the country. This was achieved through secondary legislation under the Social Security Act in the autumn of 1995, and brought into effect from February 1996. It is estimated that 10,000 asylum-seekers were forced to sleep in church halls or with friends, dependent for food on charities and food parcels, as a result of this measure (Mills, 1996).

The government was forced to resume payment of benefits in June, following a ruling by the Court of Appeal that it had acted outside its powers under the Social Security Act. However, it was then decided to use the Asylum and Immigration Act to introduce clauses confirming the secondary legislation, which was done at the very end of the parliamentary session.

When benefits were again removed in July, there was a further challenge in the courts on the grounds that councils were legally required to provide shelter and subsistence to asylum-seekers under the 1948 National Assistance Act. One civil servant I interviewed observed that, in the rush to get the 1995 Bill enacted before the end of the parliamentary session, the existence of the 1948 Act had been overlooked by the team who had drafted the new clauses:

> "Whoever drafted the legislation – legal advisors, parliamentary draughtsmen, ministers, officials – between them, not one of them picked it up that there was this requirement in the 1948 Act. I mean there are so many Acts aren't there – who knows how many of them are active or not? You can see how it happens ... but I think someone bungled on this one.... It was the kind of thing that could have been put to bed very easily if they'd found that section in the 1948 Act. It would have been simply scheduled to the Bill, among all the other bits and pieces that are repealed in this section – s21 National Assistance Act 1948. No one would have given this a second thought.
>
> Precious few people would have gone to each of those to see exactly what that is, and if they had gone to it, they would have seen that it was entirely consistent with what the government

was proposing, which was that these people should not get recourse to public funds. They weren't proposing just benefits, they were proposing ... to reduce the incentives for people to claim asylum. And that would apply just as much to shelters provided by local authorities, as it would to putting 40 quid in your hand every week down at the benefit office."

The net-result of the attempt to remove benefits was that only some asylum-seekers suffered hardship, given that it was still possible to obtain full benefits by claiming asylum immediately on arrival at the airport. From the perspective of the Home Office, the whole exercise was successful in that it resulted in a substantial fall in new asylum claims.

The Short-Procedure

Another way in which the Home Office tried to reduce the backlog was through making changes to the initial decision-making process. They introduced a pilot scheme known as 'the Short-Procedure', which has since been extended to cover most categories of asylum applicants (Jagmohan, 1996). In the old system, applicants had been given a self-completion questionnaire in which they could give their reasons for claiming asylum in their own words. After receipt of the completed questionnaire, the asylum-seeker would normally be interviewed at a later date. Under the new procedure, they were not given the questionnaire, but were invited to submit further representations after the interview. The pilot scheme found that interviews were, on average, quicker, despite the absence of the questionnaire. The delay between completion of the asylum interview and reaching a decision on the application was also reduced.

The drafting of the 1995 Asylum and Immigration Bill

The 1995 Asylum and Immigration Bill was introduced into Parliament for its first reading, without any prior consultation with pressure groups or other political parties in November 1995. The sections of the Act concerned with the appeals process gave the government power to 'certify' or 'designate' appeals from countries it viewed as 'safe' (the so-called 'white list'), or in a number of other circumstances such as where false documents had been used to obtain entry to the United Kingdom[6]. These would be heard in a separate accelerated appeals system, with the objective of speeding up the initial determination and appeals process for large numbers of 'routine' claims[7]. The Bill also contained clauses that imposed penalties on businesses for employing illegal immigrants, and made 'racketeering' a criminal offence.

The variety of measures proposed in the Bill originated in discussions which took place between civil servants and ministers in the autumn of 1994. One interviewee provided some insight into the kind of process involved at this stage of the Bill (and also into the relationship between ministers and civil servants):

> MT: **Was the Bill what you wanted?**
>
> A1: **There was a considerable amount of pressure from ministers ... (1) to do something about the increased number of asylum-seekers, and (2) to do something in particular about illegal working. And so a Bill itself was largely what we wanted as officials to cope with additional applications, and in the end of the day that got minister's approval, and the illegal working bit was also something that ministers in particular wanted, so, as a Bill, it didn't cause us any problems.**
>
> **And, at the end of the day, whether it caused us problems or not is neither here nor there, because if ministers want that legislation in a particular form, it's our duty to try to give it to them in that form, and to assist them in getting it through Parliament in that form.**
>
> MT: **You mean, there could have been more in it?**
>
> A1: **Yes, but from the civil service point of view, the point is to identify what ministers want to do. We say, 'OK you want to do this. Then here's how you can do it. There's a range of options'.**

The package of measures chosen were those which ministers felt had the best chance of getting through cabinet, in view of the fact that every other government department would also be putting forward a bid for parliamentary time. The Home Office was successful in making a bid for a legislative slot in December 1994 for the parliamentary session starting in November 1995.

It is difficult to reconstruct the work involved in drafting the Bill since, by the time I interviewed civil servants in the Home Office in 1997, the Bill team that had been set up in 1995 had been disbanded. Most of the civil servants who had worked on the Bill had moved to different sections. They would have consulted with interested parties in the Home Office, and other government departments over several months, as well as with parliamentary draughtsmen, to produce the document which was introduced into parliament. According to one member of this team:

> "There was a tremendous amount of work, because not only were we taking our own interests into account, but we are taking the interests of a range of other government departments, and making sure that our legislation is not going to impinge on any of their activities. And also we are taking their views into account."

All this work took place before the Bill was laid before Parliament in November 1995.

The passage of the Bill

The process of steering the Asylum and Immigration Bill through Parliament also involved a great deal of work on the part of civil servants and ministers. Any Bill has to progress through a number of standard stages before it becomes law. It is introduced into the House of Commons for a first and second reading, considered in committee, sent to the House of Lords, and then returned to the Commons. From the point of view of civil servants and ministers, the central objective was for all these stages to be completed within a year. If the opposition managed to delay matters, or parliamentary time had to be used for other things, the Bill would have to be introduced afresh in the next parliamentary session.

By the time, I interviewed the civil servants involved, the Bill was already past history, and it was difficult to reconstruct the negotiations which had taken place inside Parliament. A comment by one civil servant, about the introduction of the benefits clauses into the Bill, illustrates how people at work are most interested in their own tasks and problems:

> "I forget what the details were. All I know is that it was nothing to do with my section. I think it was about sections 10, 11 and

12 ... [turns to other civil servant] the DSS regulations? Yes, it was. There was a court judgment against them, against the DSS."

Because the government wanted to introduce the measures in this Bill quickly, it agreed to a late amendment, giving additional protection to victims of torture. The House of Lords were, however, unsuccessful in proposing another amendment, at the eleventh hour, which would have extended the period in which one could claim asylum, and still be entitled to benefits, to three days after arriving at a port or airport.

Assessing the Act

According to the civil servants I interviewed, it was still far too early in the summer of 1997 to assess whether the Act had been successful in achieving its objectives. They knew from the outset that the accelerated listing of certified cases (six to seven weeks as against 70 weeks) could only be achieved by causing greater delays in hearing other appeals, owing to the overall lack of resources in the appeals system. However, this was seen as a price worth paying:

> "If you put it this way, if you don't have designated cases, you might find you'd only got 68 rather than 70 weeks listing every appeal. It might come down by a few weeks. But, this way, cases are dealt with quickly that are likely to have less merit, because they are from countries which are considered safe. They are still considered on their individual merits, but once listed, they are heard quickly, and so can be removed more quickly. This will hopefully act as a discouragement to people thinking of coming here to claim asylum [to get benefits] because it doesn't work. Whereas it shouldn't affect the genuine asylum-seeker because it doesn't matter to them if their case is heard sooner or later."

The civil servants I interviewed also told me that it might take a few years to know if the provisions relating to employment had any effect in identifying illegal immigrants. It was still unclear whether the Labour government would want to implement this part of the Act.

The making of the 1996 procedural rules

While the passage of the 1996 Asylum and Immigration Act was generating debate in Parliament and the media, a great deal of behind-the-scenes work was taking place to agree the new procedural rules which came into effect in September 1996. I will begin by describing the nature and purpose of the rules which govern courts and tribunals, and then try to reconstruct some of the discussion that took place between different organisations in this court-system in 1996. This will provide a further insight into the nature of different institutional perspectives in the immigration courts (a central theme in this study), and also into another aspect of the routine, clerical work which is involved in the administration of justice.

The need for procedural rules

Courts are complex organisations in which a range of groups and individuals collaborate to secure outcomes for particular individuals who seek to use the judicial process, or, in criminal cases, are brought unwillingly before a judge and jury by the organised power of the state. The law itself can be viewed as a public set of rules instructing decision makers how to reach decisions in particular circumstances, and there are also secondary rules in most court-systems which govern what can be introduced as evidence, and how hearings should be conducted. In addition, all courts and tribunals require a set of procedural rules, instructing court-users about the workings of the system.

The rules currently governing asylum appeals are set out in a 16-page booklet called the 1996 Asylum Appeals (Procedure) Rules[8]. These replaced the 1993 Asylum Appeals (Procedure) Rules, which were in force from 1993-96. Immigration appeals are still governed by a set of rules brought into force in 1984. A policy unit in the Lord Chancellor's Department is responsible for reviewing the operation of these rules.

According to a civil servant in this unit, even a court-system that had relatively informal rules of evidence required a detailed set of procedural rules:

> "It's got to make it clear to everyone how you lodge the appeal, whether there's a time limit, what kind of information you have to give at that stage. It then has to tell you who's going to be on the tribunal, how it's going to be composed. It then has

> to tell you what you can expect from the other side, what's
> going to happen at the hearing, and what you can expect
> afterwards, and what further avenues of appeal you might have.
>
> Well, that might be only a short list, but when you try to provide
> explanations that take account of various variations on a theme,
> it gets to be quite lengthy."

Drafting the 1996 rules was, itself, a lengthy and complex administrative
task in which the Lord Chancellor's Department consulted different groups
in the court-system. I will now discuss the origins of the new rules in
the 1994 KPMG report, and the process of making the new rules, and
then examine the perspective of the different institutions involved.

The recommendations of the 1994 KPMG report

The decision to make a new set of procedural rules in 1996 was partly a
consequence of the recommendations made by the management
consultants KPMG in 1994 "into difficulties experienced in operating
the Asylum Appeals (Procedure) Rules 1993". They were jointly
commissioned by the Lord Chancellor's Department and the Home Office
to investigate whether it was possible to improve the efficiency of the
appeals process, in view of the growing backlog.

None of the civil servants I interviewed were in post at the time when
the KPMG report was commissioned, although they were used to the
idea of government departments using firms of management consultants
to address administrative problems. They described this report in the
following terms:

A1: KPMG didn't go in and produce a complete blueprint. They
     produced some ideas that were implemented, and they
     produced some ideas which, on examination, turned out
     to be pretty dud.

A2: It wasn't a big deal. It wasn't the immigration tribunal's
     version of the Woolf Report. It was kind of a health check,
     and it had all the strengths and weaknesses of a consultant's
     report.... You know Harvey Jones' definition of a consultant
     is someone who follows you around to tell you what the

> **time is, and there was a certain element of that in it. But
> you always get that with a management consultant's report.**

In an examination of 214 appeals, KPMG found that the time limits set
down in the 1993 rules for determining appeals were being missed in a
large number of cases. They identified one cause of delay in the large
number of appeals which were adjourned, sometimes on more than one
occasion. Common reasons for adjournments included illness on the
part of the appellant, and the fact that the appellant's representative was
not ready for the hearing.

In response to these problems, KPMG recommended that adjudicators
should be given more powers to require parties to prepare for hearings
by giving directions, with the sanction that, if they did not comply, they
could hear the appeal without all the evidence. They also wanted
adjudicators to have the power to impose cost orders on firms that sought
"unnecessary last minute adjournments", or "who put forward a frivolous
application for leave to appeal to the tribunal simply as a way of spinning
out the process for a client who had been unsuccessful at the appeal
stage" (KPMG, 1994, p 35). They also noted, however, that "none of
these powers...will have any effect unless the judiciary is willing to use
them and enforce their powers"[9].

The process of rule making

Even without the KPMG report, it is likely that the Lord Chancellor's
Department would have revised the 1993 rules, acting on suggestions
from different parties in the court-system. The process of making the
rules took about a year, between September 1995 and August 1996, and
involved a lengthy period of consultation with different groups, with
ministers kept informed on how they were developing.

The first stage of the consultation process took place in the autumn of
1995, when drafts were circulated to the organisations most directly
affected, such as the Immigration Appellate Authority, and the Home
Office. A draft incorporating their suggestions was then given to the
Council on Tribunals, a statutory body which has the task of reviewing
the operation of tribunals for the government. Having received their
comments, a copy of the rules was sent out to a wider range of court-
users, including the IAS, the Refugee Legal Centre, the Law Society, the
Bar, Asylum Aid, and the Immigration Law Practitioners' Association
(ILPA). The Home Office and Immigration Appellate Authority then

responded to their suggestions, and after some toing and froing, a final version was agreed in early summer. They were laid before Parliament on 7 August, and came into force on 1 September.

Different perspectives on the rules

Although most parties were satisfied with the eventual result, it seems evident that disagreements did emerge during the drafting, which illustrate the nature of different institutional perspectives in this court-system. One civil servant, who had become involved in the final stages of the consultative process, explained how problems could emerge in the following terms:

> "Because of ... the complexity of some of the issues, there was a good deal of consultation I had to go through with the rules, with people like the Council on Tribunals, and the immigration adjudicators themselves. And, inevitably – and I was neither surprised nor disappointed by this – you get different perspectives. Somehow you have to find the right balance between different interests."

Although it is difficult, retrospectively, to reconstruct the detailed discussion which took place during this consultative process, my interviews do give some insight into what different institutions wanted from the rules.

The Home Office and the rules

The Home Office saw the rules as another opportunity, in conjunction with the other measures I have described in this chapter, to reduce the backlog in the court-system. It is evident from comparing the 1993 and 1996 rules that some rule changes were intended to reduce delays in the appeals process. Consider, for example, the rule giving adjudicators power to adjourn hearings. In the 1993 rules, this stated: "a special adjudicator may grant an application for an adjournment upon being satisfied that there is good cause for the adjournment." In the 1996 rules, this had become: "a special adjudicator shall not adjourn a hearing unless he is satisfied that an adjournment is necessary for the just disposal of the appeal".

Some of the Presenting Officers I spoke to felt that this kind of clause could have been worded in considerably stronger terms, which would make it difficult for adjudicators to adjourn hearings, or for The Tribunal to 'remit' cases back to adjudicators.

Adjudicators and the rules

Adjudicators wanted to retain their freedom of action against outside interference or direction from the Home Office. The Lord Chancellor's Department also saw its role as defending the independence of the judiciary. It would, for example, have been possible to devise a rule which compelled adjudicators to adjourn less appeals. However, as one civil servant observed:

> **"I think to put it in a way that is stronger than it already is would be an intrusion on judicial discretion. You can't tell the judiciary what to do. They have to decide in the circumstances of every individual case."**

The Council on Tribunals and the rules

The Council on Tribunals submits an annual report to Parliament about tribunals under its supervision, and the 1996 report indicates that it was concerned about a reduction in the time allowed to appellants for submitting a 'notice of appeal'. It also wanted the new rules to relax the tight time limits in the 1993 rules, because these had become unrealistic owing to the backlog. In this case, the Lord Chancellor's Department felt unable to accept their recommendation, but it did agree to monitor the operation of the time limits, and report back to the Council:

> **"One of the points they were quite concerned about was the maintenance of tight time limits for asylum appeals, so we gave an undertaking that we'd review the time limits again a certain period after the Act and the new rules had been in place, and for some of the new procedures we were bringing in, that adjudicators perhaps hadn't had before. We agreed that we would set up a system of monitoring to make sure that they weren't having a detrimental effect on appellants. So even though we were not able to adopt every piece of advice they gave us, we did listen to it very carefully, and tried to find ways that we might keep a check on ourselves."**

Other court-users

The main concern of some of the other organisations consulted about the rules – which included the IAS and the Refugee Legal Centre – was that they should strike a fair balance between the interests of the appellant and the government. If, for example, representatives for the appellant were required to submit documents at a certain time before the hearing, they wanted the same requirement to be placed on the Home Office[10].

From the point of view of the Home Office, this kind of proposal was undesirable, because it would lead to further delays in the appeals process. One interviewee explained his objection in the following terms:

> **"Yes, there was a debate at some point over whether the Home Office should be required to supply documents if adjudicators or The Tribunal said they should, and this was strongly resisted by the Home Office, so it doesn't appear in them. The Lord Chancellor's Department said it has to affect both sides, so if [an adjudicator] demands something from the appellant he has got to produce it, and if he demands something from the Home Office, we have got to produce it. Now the Lord Chancellor's Department's view is that's fair to both sides, and we need to run a system that is fair to both sides. The Home Office view will be that, in practice, in every case, the other side will start demanding to see the documents.... And this will be another opportunity to delay the process."**

It seems likely that some horse-trading may have taken place in determining the final content of the rules. The Home Secretary and Lord Chancellor may ultimately have been asked to resolve any outstanding areas that could not be agreed at a lower level in the civil service. Although no one got everything they wanted, it appeared that, by the summer of 1996, all the parties were satisfied with the content of the rules.

The effect on organisations

Although I have emphasised the role of the civil service, it is important to remember that every organisation in the court-system also had to deal with the problem of the backlog, as a practical and pressing concern. Managers were under considerable pressure to increase efficiency, and process larger numbers of appellants, or risk losing their funding from the Home Office or Lord Chancellor's Department. Practitioners found that their day-to-day work was affected by these initiatives, and the 1996 Act and Rules. I will now describe how these changes affected three organisations: the Immigration Advisory Service; a Unit of Home Office Presenting Officers; and the Immigration Appellate Authority.

The Immigration Advisory Service

The IAS was undergoing a rapid period of expansion, and internal reorganisation, while I was doing my fieldwork. Its chief officer, Keith Best, was successful in bidding for part of the Spend-to-Save money administered by the Home Office, which allowed him to recruit additional counsellors, and open a new floor of offices in the London headquarters of the organisation. However, this investment was conditional on the IAS meeting higher targets in the number of clients it advised and represented each financial year.

When I started my fieldwork, the IAS were still awaiting the results of their application for Spend-to-Save money. In some regional offices, counsellors were refusing to take on new clients, because they felt that they were unable to prepare appeals to the standards they wished, without using their own time. Managers were, however, trying to persuade them to spend less time establishing rapport with clients, or researching the law in depth. It was, in their view, possible to offer an acceptable level of service by spending less time on each appeal.

Further demands on counsellors were made by the new Procedural Rules which required representatives to submit skeleton arguments and witness statements prior to the appeal, with the aim of reducing the length of the hearing. The solution adopted by the organisation was to invest in personal computers for each counsellor, while reducing the ratio of counsellors to secretarial staff. Counsellors were asked to type their own correspondence and documents relating to their case-work.

Home Office Presenting Officers

Presenting Officers were also preparing themselves for significant changes in the way they worked as a result of the introduction of new technology. Everyone had, for example, been informed that 1,200 posts were likely to disappear in the Immigration and Nationality Department in the next five years, through the introduction of a system which would allow case-workers to handle a mixture of asylum and immigration appeals.

The civil servants I interviewed expressed similar views to IAS counsellors about the effect of an increasing case-load on the quality of their work. Some complained that they did not want to look foolish in court in front of adjudicators, as a result of being unprepared. In addition, they also had a strong sense of professional identity based on providing the best possible service to clients. In each organisation, individuals told similar stories about how they had to work late at night, because they did not have enough time to prepare appeals adequately during the day[11].

One proposal that was being discussed in early 1997 was that Presenting Officers should no longer cross-examine, or make a closing submission, in certain kinds of routine appeals. Instead of presenting the government's case, the Presenting Officer would simply invite the adjudicator to assess the evidence presented by the appellant's representative. Some felt that this might be justified in the interests of saving resources, even if it meant losing a few more appeals.

The Immigration Appellate Authority

Because they were judicial officials, adjudicators were effectively free of direct pressure from managers, or civil servants, although the Chief Adjudicator and President of The Tribunal were expected to monitor how individuals made adjournments, and managed hearings. Instead, common practices arose through collegial discussion at meetings and training days, and there was no requirement for everyone to follow the same line.

At one meeting I attended, an adjudicator was invited to share her thoughts about how to make maximum use of the new procedural rules to reduce the length of hearings and to combat adjournments. She described how she adopted a tough policy towards requiring representatives to submit all documentation before the hearing, and to limit the length of submissions and the time allowed for examination-in-chief and cross-examination. She had also adopted the practice, which was permitted under the rules, of announcing the determination orally at the end of the hearing for most appeals. Finally, she felt that the definition of determinations in the new rules made it possible to omit a detailed discussion of the law, and reduce the average length from 10 to four pages. It was now possible to type or dictate the determination on the day of the hearing, and determine three or four appeals on each day in court.

This adjudicator described herself as a "voice in the wilderness", in that most of her colleagues were not taking advantage of rules in this way. Some adjudicators expressed similar sentiments to IAS counsellors and Presenting Officers to the effect that the pressure on them to clear up the backlog had potential implications for the quality of their work. According to one informant, many new adjudicators were reluctant to hear more than two appeals in any one day, because they took longer in writing up their determinations, and were sensitive about making mistakes that might result in their decisions being appealed:

> "You're dealing with a lot of very new, both full-time and part-time adjudicators, who are on a large learning curve, and who themselves feel unable to sit right through a whole day hearing evidence, without sort of addling their brain. In any event, they need the time to write up their determinations. The case may be a very short one in terms of evidence, it may last only an hour, but if there's lots of law in it ... it can take a very long time writing the determination to make sure you don't get taken up to the Immigration Appeal Tribunal because there's some defect in the process. So, you'll find there is a reluctance among adjudicators to sit very long."

This comment indicates that the appointment of new personnel did not necessarily enable the courts to hear more appeals, at least in the short term. While I was doing my fieldwork, some hearing rooms were staffed by new adjudicators, counsellors and Presenting Officers, all learning the job through a process of trial and error, with frequent adjournments by adjudicators to consult with more experienced colleagues. Given these circumstances, it would take some time before the investment of new resources from the Spend-to-Save money could be expected to have much effect in increasing the flow of cases through the courts.

The 1999 Immigration and Asylum Act

Despite all the efforts made during the period 1994-96, the civil servants responsible for the court-system were aware that much more needed to be done before there could be a significant reduction in the backlog. By the end of 1996, there were still long delays for many appellants in the decision-making and appeals process, and the majority of these were still entitled to claim social security and other benefits despite the measures taken in the 1996 Act.

By the end of 1996, it also seems clear that ministers in the Conservative government remained unhappy about the continuing problems in the courts. To the surprise of many organisations in the court-system, there was an announcement in the House of Commons that a review of the appeal procedures would take place during 1997. After winning power in the May 1997 general election, the new Labour government announced that it had commissioned a wider review, which would be published in the autumn. This was not completed until the following August, when the government published a White Paper on immigration and asylum policy (Home Office, 1998). This pledged that all initial decisions and appeals would take place within six months of any asylum claim by the end of 2001. The 1999 Immigration and Asylum Bill was introduced into the House of Commons in February 1999, and will become law, subject to any revisions during the parliamentary process, shortly after this book is published.

The 1999 Bill is a much longer piece of legislation than the 1996 Act, and makes a number of important changes to the immigration court-system. The most controversial measure is likely to be a new system of cashless support, to be administered by the Home Office, in which asylum-seekers will be required to live in 'designated' reception centres around the country, in order to relieve the pressure on London councils. The court-system itself is not substantially changed, although the Bill establishes a 'one-stop appeals' system, which is designed to reduce the length of the appeals process (particularly for over-stayers who claim asylum in order to postpone being deported). It also restores the right of appeal for visitors, which was removed by the 1993 Act, although there will be an administrative charge.

There are, of course, many other important clauses in the Bill which are not directly relevant to this study. One set of measures is intended to strengthen pre-entry controls. The 1987 Immigration (Carriers' Liability) Act imposed a £2,000 fine on airlines for each passenger who arrives without proper documentation. This has so far had only a limited success, except as a means of generating revenue, but it is now proposed to send teams of Airline Liaison Officers to work with carriers, in the hope of preventing people who might later claim asylum from travelling to the United Kingdom.

Another politically controversial measure is that checks at airports will be reduced, but that immigration officers will be given more investigative powers to combat illegal immigration. This may result in a move towards the kind of internal controls used on the continent, where every citizen is issued with an identity card.

The intractable character of an administrative problem

If the civil service is successful in achieving the target promised in the Labour government's 1998 White Paper, it will have accomplished what the Wilson Report intended in 1968: a speedy but fair system of determining appeals, which will make it easier to remove unsuccessful applicants. As this book goes to press, most practitioners seem doubtful that this will occur, particularly since decision making in the Home Office has completely broken down owing to problems in introducing a new computer system in Lunar House. Despite all the measures taken by the civil service, and other organisations, everyone knows that the backlog will remain a significant problem for the foreseeable future. This is because there are only a limited number of options that can be taken by any government in relation to immigration policy or the appeals system.

The most obvious solution – to spend more money – is simply unacceptable at a time when all government spending departments are competing for reduced resources. Other radical policy measures, such as giving more applicants Exceptional Leave to Remain, or, alternatively, withdrawing from the 1951 Convention altogether, would also not be entertained by any politically-sensitive government. This leaves the administrative and legislative measures which have been reviewed in this chapter. These attempt to improve the speed of the appeals process, without spending substantially more resources on the courts[12].

Although moves are being taken to encourage adjudicators to reduce the length of hearings, it would be viewed as politically unacceptable if the government abolished a right to an oral hearing for asylum appellants. For one thing, any appellant could then apply for Judicial Review, which takes considerably longer than the normal appeals process. In this respect, the difference of perspective between the Home Office and Lord Chancellor's Department becomes significant. As one civil servant observed:

> "The Home Office point of view ... is to be fair, but it is to recognise that there is a considerable volume of cases in which justice needs to be done, and to achieve that as expeditiously and effectively as possible.... The tension on that is, you try to get things done as quickly as you can, you tend to eat into what you consider justice.
>
> Now, of course, in all jurisdictions when the Home Office comes into contact with the Lord Chancellor's Department, tension

will come from the Home Office taking what I would call a practical view – 'You've only got so much money' – and the Lord Chancellor's Department, quite rightly, taking a sort of absolutist view, the pure justice view, 'These are judges. This is the way they operate. You can't rush them. There have to be certain, absolutely guaranteed elements which guarantee their independence. They can't be forced to do 20 cases in a day because they need time for proper reflection...'.

And that is the fundamental tension that runs between the Home Office and the Lord Chancellor's Department across all these jurisdictions. And it's probably right that we have that tension, whereas some countries just have a Ministry of Justice in which the whole thing is swallowed up in one department."

A good example of how the Home Office was prevented from getting its own way in reducing costs was the fate of a recommendation in 1980 by the Home Secretary to remove the funding which supported publication of the Green Books, the series reporting important immigration appeals. This was apparently dropped following representations from the Council on Tribunals.

The extent to which the Lord Chancellor's Department can guarantee standards of justice is, of course, itself constrained by the resources it obtains from the rest of government. One policy debate, which I have not yet mentioned in this chapter, is the question of whether legal aid should cover representation at hearings.

This is regularly raised by organisations like the Immigration Law Practitioners' Association, and the Lord Chancellor's Department has already commissioned one academic study which suggests that there is a connection between the quality of representation, and the outcome for appellants across a wide range of tribunals (Genn and Genn, 1983)[13]. The 1996 Green Paper on Legal Aid again considered whether legal aid should be extended to tribunals, but decided that this should be given low priority as a policy objective.

There are two main reasons why civil servants are reluctant to extend legal aid to tribunals. In the first place, some still support the original philosophy behind the 1957 Franks Report which intended tribunals to be less formal than proper courts. Even if it is acknowledged that the immigration courts do not operate in this way, there is, however, still the issue of cost. One interviewee's response to critics who suggest that more money should be spent on the courts conveys this view particularly clearly:

> **"I bet they weren't too hot in suggesting areas in which legal aid should be withdrawn to pay for it. That's the dilemma. Or, indeed, what other areas of public spending should be reduced to pay for the legal aid itself."**

These dilemmas concerning the relationship between the judiciary and the executive, and the cost of supporting high quality services out of shrinking revenues, have faced successive British governments who have wanted to establish a fair but effective system of immigration control.

Notes

[1] There is some discussion of the importance of administrative work in Feeley (1979) and Rock (1993).

[2] According to one interviewee, it was a "typical fast-streamer's fallacy" to assume that most people in the civil service were engaged in making policy. In his view, very few policy initiatives had much effect on the day-to-day work of the civil service.

[3] For discussion of the 1993 Asylum and Immigration Act, see Randall (1994).

[4] There was a backlog of 52,000 asylum applications in May 1998, 10,000 of which were over five years old (Home Office, 1998, p 16).

[5] See the *Report of the Social Security Committee of the House of Commons on Benefits for Asylum Seekers* (1996).

[6] The countries on the 'white list' were Bulgaria, Cyprus, Ghana, India, Pakistan, Poland and Romania.

[7] Although critics claimed that this new way of hearing appeals would inevitably be biased, there is, in fact, no real difference between the task of adjudicators in 'certified' or ordinary appeals. The Act extended the accelerated appeals process established by the 1993 Asylum and Immigration Act to a wider range of refused asylum applications, which are heard in a new hearing centre at Lincoln House in London. Under this accelerated process, the Immigration Appellate Authority

is required to apply shorter time-limits in disposing of these appeals, and if the certificate of the Home Secretary certifying the appeal for the accelerated procedure is upheld by the adjudicator, there is no right to seek leave to appeal to The Tribunal. As it turned out, the volume of work quickly made the new time-limits unworkable, and the system of certifying appeals has started to create its own backlog.

[8] A new set of rules is currently being drafted which will come into effect on the enactment of the 1999 Immigration and Asylum Act.

[9] They suggest that one way to achieve this would be by spending more time training adjudicators to adopt a tougher line towards adjournments.

[10] Some of the rules were subsequently challenged through Judicial Review during 1998, but were found to be *intra vires*. The High Court rejected the view that they were in breach of natural justice, through denying the appellant a fair hearing.

[11] The problems faced by these groups are shared by many other occupations at a time of cut-backs in the public sector, such as teachers, doctors, nurses, and social workers. See Lipsky (1980) for an analysis of similar issues facing American public sector workers in the 1970s.

[12] Perhaps the major concern driving policy has been an attempt to reduce the cost of supporting asylum-seekers before their appeal hearing, which is far greater than the cost of the determination and appeals system. Social security payments to asylum-seekers were estimated at £200 million per annum before 1996. The asylum system now costs more than £500 million a year, despite the removal of benefits, of which £400 million is spent on "direct support and other costs such as health and education" (Home Office, 1998, p 17). One civil servant told me that it cost £40 million per annum in 1996 to run the courts, which covered the salary bill for adjudicators and administrative staff.

[13] This report found that represented appellants were more successful in winning their appeals, through a statistical analysis of a number of tribunals. It has, however, been criticised for not sufficiently taking into account other variables which might explain outcomes. See Young (1990).

SEVEN

Immigration as a political issue

Immigration has not simply been an administrative problem for the civil service: it has also featured regularly as an issue which has raised passions, and generated debate, in national political life. In this chapter, I will look at the history of this issue in post-war British politics, drawing upon the accounts supplied by Saggar (1992) and Layton-Henry (1984), and discuss the work of politicians, pressure groups and campaigners. I will also examine the content of political debate in Parliament during the passage of the 1996 Asylum and Immigration Act, and review the proposals that have been put forward to change British immigration policy in recent years.

The history of immigration as a political issue

Immigration became an important issue in post-war British politics in the 1950s, when pressure began to build up on the Conservative Party to retreat from its commitment to open borders in the newly formed Commonwealth. This was led by a small group of maverick backbench MPs, including Cyril Osborne who introduced a Private Member's Bill into the House of Commons advocating immigration controls in February 1961. The 1962 Commonwealth Immigrants Act was partly the result of Conservative ministers bowing to irresistible political pressure from their own grass roots.

The Labour Party leadership also changed its policy towards controls following the 1964 General Election, when Patrick Gordon-Walker, the Shadow Foreign Secretary, lost his seat to Peter Griffiths who fought a campaign against Labour's 'softness' on the immigration issue. This shift in policy resulted in the 1968 Commonwealth Immigrants Act, and cross-Party agreement on the need for stricter immigration controls. As Saggar observes:

> **The new mood first reached across the different strands of thought in the Labour Party and then embraced both major parties. The consensus aimed to keep political debate concerning race and immigration to questions of *means* rather than *ends*,**

> **with both major parties agreeing that prior restriction of Commonwealth immigration was a necessary precondition for harmonious race relations. (Saggar, 1992, p 77)**

Despite this consensus, immigration continued to pose a problem for both political parties during the 1970s. One reason why the Labour Party lost the election in 1970 may have been that it was still perceived as being 'weak' on immigration control, at a time when public concern was continuing to rise. According to Saggar, "the Conservative's electoral edge over Labour as the tougher party on immigration grew steadily from 13 points in 1966 to 53 points by 1970", despite the 1968 Commonwealth Immigrants Act. Enoch Powell's calls for repatriation in the 'rivers of blood' speech in 1968 may also have contributed to the Conservatives' victory in 1970, even though he was sacked from the Shadow cabinet by Edward Heath.

The Heath government also ran into difficulties on immigration, through sending out contradictory messages to the electorate. It began by enacting the tough 1971 Immigration Act, but then gave way to pressure from those arguing that Britain should honour its imperial obligations, when it came to admitting 50,000 Ugandan Asians. This may have been one factor in its defeat in 1974.

The Labour government from 1974–79 fared little better. Despite breaking an electoral promise to repeal the 1971 Immigration Act, it also came to be perceived as 'soft' on immigration. This was exploited, firstly by the National Front, and then by Margaret Thatcher, who told viewers of the Granada television programme World in Action in 1978, that Britain was being "swamped" by people from "alien cultures". It is difficult to assess the significance of this issue in securing the Conservatives' victory in the 1979 General Election, although opinion polls (or at least those reported in the *Daily Mail*) indicated a 9% rise in the Party's rating after the interview (Saggar, 1992, p 250).

After the enactment of the 1981 British Nationality Act, immigration quickly became something of a non-issue in electoral terms, despite the fact that the Conservative Party introduced the Immigration (Carrier's Liability) Bill, and the first Asylum and Immigration Bill, shortly before the 1987 and 1992 general elections. According to Saggar, the 1981 Act defused the radical Right, who never went on to call for repatriation by the Conservative government. He also notes that "the actual scale of immigration declined sharply in the early 1980s and has remained low ever since" (Saggar, 1992, p 128).

In the 1983 election, Crewe found that "immigration ... dropped off the political agenda" (Saggar, 1992, p 128), and there is similar evidence that the issue was of little importance to voters in 1987 (Law, 1996, p x). Asylum became an issue for politicians and the media in the early 1990s, but there is no evidence that this influenced voters in the 1993 or 1997 elections. Immigration has, arguably, lost its force as the kind of issue that can make a difference in general elections, particularly since there is now little difference between the policies of the main parties on either immigration or asylum[1].

Politicians, pressure groups and campaigners

Politics can be broadly defined as any activity that seeks to influence government policy in managing social and economic life. Policy is made through the political process, in the course of a complex interaction between decision makers, such as government ministers, civil servants, and Members of Parliament, and the general public. Three types of political work were being pursued during my fieldwork which were concerned with influencing government policy concerning immigration and asylum. These were the work of professional politicians, pressure groups, and campaigners.

The work of professional politicians

Decision making in Britain, and other democratic countries, is organised through a system in which electorates vote for politicians at national elections. The competition between political parties is central to this process. The government of the day will attempt to use the media, and parliamentary process, to persuade the public that it deserves to be re-elected. The opposition, on the other hand, will attempt to expose the failings of the government in different areas of policy, and secure power for itself in the next election.

To understand the day-to-day work of politicians, it is necessary to distinguish between ministers and Members of Parliament. Ministers are responsible for putting manifesto promises into effect, through managing government departments, and presenting policy to the public[2]. The current immigration minister at the Home Office is Mike O'Brien, who reports to the Home Secretary Jack Straw. His responsibilities include consulting with pressure groups, and answering questions from the floor at public meetings.

Members of Parliament relay the concerns of members of the public to ministers, through their representation of constituencies. During the 1960s and 1970s, grass-roots feeling in the country against immigration was a key factor in the development of more restrictive policies. They also play an important role during the passage of legislation through Parliament. Little academic research has so far been conducted on their day-to-day work, or the procedural tactics used to obtain party advantage during the legislative process.

The work of pressure groups

There are a large number of pressure groups seeking to influence this area of government policy. These were particularly active in 1996, when opposition to the Conservative government's Asylum and Immigration Bill was supported outside Parliament by a coalition which included civil rights organisations like Justice and Amnesty International, practitioners' groups like the Immigration Law Practitioners' Association, the churches, community organisations, local authorities, and organisations representing refugees. This coalition organised two demonstrations in London in March and April 1996, and a panel in London under the chairmanship of Sir Iain Glidewell, a retired Court of Appeal judge, which took evidence in public sessions held in February and March 1996, and presented a set of recommendations to the government[3]. It also organised public meetings around the country, which were intended to generate public opposition to the Bill.

Pressure groups were also responsible for the steady stream of reports about asylum-seekers, and immigration more generally, which appeared in the media during the 1995-96 parliamentary session. Different newspapers have a distinctive editorial bias, which influences their selection and presentation of stories. The *Daily Mail* has published many reports and editorials about 'bogus' asylum-seekers, and has campaigned for a 'firmer and faster' appeals process. These often draw upon press releases issued by the Home Office, and the Immigration Service Union, a pressure group which favours greater controls.

On the opposite side of the political spectrum, liberal papers, like *The Guardian* and *The Independent*, publish reports which are more sympathetic towards asylum-seekers. They often support campaigns by individuals affected by immigration control, and draw upon press releases supplied by pressure groups like Justice and Amnesty International.

As well as trying to get favourable stories in the media, pressure groups also attempt to educate decision makers about factual issues, and counter disinformation put out by the government. One interviewee described this in the following terms:

> **"What you are trying to do is provide information to people so that they are informed and make the decisions that you believe are the correct ones.... So, if MPs get a question from a constituent or whatever, they say 'Oh, I've read your briefing, and you say that India is a country where persecution takes place. Why do you say this? I find this difficult to believe'. And we provide them with the information.... So, they can look at what we are saying, and what the government line is, and come to a conclusion as to whether what we're saying is actually true."**

The objective of this work is to persuade some MPs to take up refugees as an issue, by putting down an adjournment debate, or an early day motion, or asking questions in Parliament. There are, however, also MPs who can be influenced to support the cause by, for example, signing early day motions. In the 1996-97 parliamentary year, MPs tabled several hundred early day motions about asylum ("That's got to be up in the top twenty in terms of parliamentary support"), and 127 MPs from all parties signed a motion asking for a full review of procedures for detaining refugees.

From this point of view, although the campaign against the 1996 Asylum and Immigration Act was unsuccessful, it did succeed in raising national awareness about the position of asylum-seekers:

> **"You could say it was depressing ... but, the other way to look at it is that we formed quite a broad cross-section of organisations and individuals who were prepared to campaign, and did campaign very vigorously against sections of the Act, and raised awareness about how badly asylum-seekers were being treated. And I think the government did not win the communication battle in trying to say that 95% of asylum-seekers were bogus."**

Another kind of political activity during this period, which is harder to research, was conducted by the leadership of different ethnic communities against the primary purpose rule. There has traditionally been a reluctance in the various groups who constitute the Asian community, in the same way as in the longer established Jewish community, to mount high profile campaigns against government policy, for fear of stirring up resentment and racial prejudice[4]. This, perhaps, explains why there was never much organised protest against the rule during the 1980s, despite its impact on large numbers of families. The only pressure group seeking to influence opinion while I was doing my fieldwork was an organisation called APART which represented white men who wished to bring in wives or fiancées from countries like the Philippines.

One imagines, however, that despite this low public profile, there continued to be discreet, behind-the-scenes lobbying by the leadership of the Asian community, MPs representing individual constituents, and pressure groups such as the Joint Council for the Welfare of Immigrants. The announcement by the Labour Party during the election campaign of 1997 that it would abolish the primary purpose rule, followed meetings with community leaders. In return, it seems clear that Labour hoped to obtain an increase in the Asian vote in certain key marginal constituencies.

The work of campaigners

A great many people are involved in campaigns against immigration policy outside the world of professional politics. There are a number of locally-based groups which have campaigned against the policy of detaining asylum-seekers, by demonstrating outside particular detention centres[5]. One group has demonstrated on the first Sunday of each month, outside the Campsfield House Detention Centre near Oxford, for the last five years. I attended a recent demonstration at which 20 people communicated their support to detainees in the exercise yard by banging loudly on the metal perimeter fence. There have been roof-top protests, and other disturbances in this centre, including an incident which resulted in the prosecution of nine West Africans for riot and violent disorder[6].

There have also been numerous campaigns by local groups in support of particular individuals who are facing deportation. The campaign which received most publicity in 1996 was organised by a millionaire businessman trying to keep his adopted son in the United Kingdom. This was reported in the national press, and television news, and was even discussed by a panel on *Question Time*. However, most campaigns are smaller, and make little impact outside their local area. They usually culminate in the delivery of a petition to the immigration minister at Lunar House.

These campaigns are only the latest examples of a long history of political protest, pursued by individuals and local communities, that started in the early 1970s (Cohen, 1994). According to one activist, they have varied immensely in terms of their size, and impact on national politics:

> "Some campaigns are no more than support groups, and help get the person psychologically through. Other campaigns are massive struggles, like really massive struggles, relatively speaking, and there are huge demonstrations, national stuff ...Viraj Mendez is the main example. Viraj lost, of course, but other campaigns have won."

Although not every campaign was successful, they had succeeded in making people aware that it was possible to make a stand against government decisions:

> "These campaigns have broken down fatalism. In the mid-1970s, someone would get a letter from the Home Office.... You would just have to get a letter, and you'd be in fear of God. Now people do come in and say, 'Give us a campaign', like they're mad. We can't just give them a campaign, they have to go and form it. That's the whole point of it all. So it has broken down fatalism, and it has bred a certain amount of confidence about resistance...."

Campaigns organised by individuals also take up a great deal of time and administrative resources in the Home Office, since ministers have to respond to petitions from local communities, and representations from MPs.

The content of political debate

To understand immigration as a political issue, it is also necessary to examine the arguments used by each side. Here I want to focus on one exchange during the debate which took place in the House of Commons on the first reading of the 1995 Asylum and Immigration Bill. I am particularly interested in the way statistics and other kinds of evidence are used in this debate, and the way immigration is presented as a moral, rather than simply administrative, issue.

The political context of the debate

The 1995 Asylum and Immigration Bill was introduced by John Major's Conservative government in the Queen's Speech in November 1995, and quickly became one of the most contentious and emotive pieces of legislation in that parliamentary session. The Bill contained the measures to speed up the determination and appeals process which I summarised in the previous chapter. The Conservative government also announced that it would remove social security benefits from anyone who did not claim asylum immediately on entering the country, from February 1996.

Jack Straw, who was then Shadow Home Secretary, told the House of Commons that Labour would vigorously oppose the Bill, which would be unfair to asylum-seekers, and ineffective in solving the government's administrative problems. The only real solution was to spend more money on the court-system, so that applications for asylum could be determined more quickly. He noted that:

> **The Home Secretary complains that the benefit bill for asylum-seekers has increased to £200 million a year. The reason for that is not so much because the number of asylum-seekers has risen as because of the time they stay while their applications and appeals are being considered.**
>
> **If the 1993 deadlines had been kept to, the benefit bill would not be £200 million but £40 million. How typical of the government that, instead of seeking to cut delays, they cut people's benefit.... (***Hansard***, 1995-96, vol 268, p 720).**

He also noted that Britain might be found to be in breach of its obligations under the Convention through removing an in-country right of appeal for "safe third country" cases, and that the withdrawal of appeal rights to The Tribunal for many applicants might "only encourage more expensive, complicated, and time-consuming appeals" through applications to the High Court for Judicial Review (*Hansard*, 1995-96, vol 268, p 719).

From the outset, Labour also concentrated its fire on the motives of the government in introducing a Bill about immigration in the year before a general election. In speech after speech, Labour MPs referred the House to comments made by Andrew Lansley, a former head of research for the Conservative Party, who had been selected as a candidate in the forthcoming election. He had been reported as saying that the issue of immigration "played particularly well in the tabloids" during the 1992 election, and that it "has more potential to hurt". The refusal of John Major to condemn this statement was presented as further evidence that the Bill was a cynical attempt to stir up racial prejudice in the hope of winning more votes, at a time when it was well behind Labour in the opinion polls.

The tactic adopted by Labour in the House of Commons was to invite the government to refer the matter to a Special Standing Committee which could take evidence from practitioners, and other interested organisations, and take the matter out of party politics. This might have meant that the Bill would not have been enacted that session, so it is, perhaps, unsurprising that ministers were unwilling to agree to this suggestion. Instead, it went through the normal procedure for scrutinising legislation in the House of Commons and House of Lords, and was 'vigorously' contested (to use the language of parliamentarians) at every stage by the opposition.

This can be contrasted with the much smoother passage of the 1999 Immigration and Asylum Act, which was introduced in February by the Labour government (in which Jack Straw has become Home Secretary), and was sent to a Special Standing Committee at which evidence was presented by different pressure groups. One important difference between the two Acts, in parliamentary terms, is that the Labour government had a large majority, and the Conservative Party supported the Bill.

An exchange during a parliamentary debate

The debate on the first reading of the Bill took place on 11 December 1995 between 3.38 pm and 10.00 pm. The report in *Hansard* gives the full text of some 30 speeches, each averaging about 10 minutes in length. The majority of contributions by Conservative MPs supported the government, by arguing that action was necessary to deter 'bogus' asylum-seekers from coming to the United Kingdom, in the interests of 'good race relations' (see also Young, 1996). On the Labour side, many MPs argued that the bill was morally objectionable, and would stir up racial prejudice, and that the matter should be referred to a standing committee.

It would require a separate chapter to do justice to this debate. Rather than trying to summarise the full range of contributions, I have chosen to present one exchange which is reported in *Hansard*. The first speaker is Diane Abbott, the Labour MP for Hackney North and Stoke Newington, who became associated with the national campaign against the Bill. She was the only MP who asked the House to be sympathetic to 'bogus' asylum-seekers who came to Britain in the hope of a better economic life. The second is by Nirj Joseph Deva, the Conservative MP for Brentford and Isleworth.

Ms Diane Abbott (Hackney, North and Stoke Newington): **I am glad to oppose this Bill, for three reasons. First, it is based on a wholly unquantified, exaggerated and apocalyptic notion of the threat that so-called bogus asylum-seekers present to the British way of life. Secondly, the provisions of this Bill and of related legislation will inevitably affect tens of thousands of British nationals purely on the basis that they are a different colour. Finally, the effect of the Bill will be cruel and inhumane, and out of all proportion to the so-called problem with which it is designed to deal.**

Conservative Members have risen to their feet one after another to talk about this so-called problem. But given Britain's size, our prosperity and our relations with many Third World countries, it is true to say that we have taken relatively few asylum-seekers.... In 1994, we took in about 42,000 refugees and asylum-seekers; that compares with Germany which took in 127,000. So how can Conservative Members jump up and claim that Britain is in danger of being flooded with refugees and asylum-seekers?

Conservative Members insist on talking as if these people leave their homes thousands of miles away on a whim, perhaps in search of benefits and a damp council flat in Hackney. On the contrary, they leave because they believe they have no option in the face of prevailing political and – yes – economic circumstances....

Conservative Members speak sneeringly of bogus asylum-seekers who want to better themselves. Is it so wrong of people to want to better themselves? Many Members of this House would not be here today if their parents and grandparents had not wished to better themselves[7].

I do not seek to extend the terms of the law governing refugees, but I think it cruel of Conservative Members of Parliament to sneer at people as if they came here merely for benefits, and were not genuinely running away from economic instability and from the growing economic gap between the First and the Third Worlds. It is the growing gap between North and South that has led to surges of economic refugees across the world. I would respect Conservative Members more if they dealt with the underlying economic issues: debt, the prices of raw materials, GATT, and trade....

If there is, indeed, a problem of people seeking refugee or asylum status to which they know they are not entitled, much of it is caused by interminable delays. If the government took administrative action to clear the 50,000 backlog and made sure that applications were dealt with quickly and efficiently, much of the incentive for unfounded claims would be removed. It is, therefore, wrong to pursue this legislation when there are administrative remedies to hand which the government have not explored.

The facts do not bear out the apocalyptic notion that the country is in danger of being swamped by millions of these people. This Bill, and the debates centering on it, which will inevitably drag on into next year, can only poison the atmosphere around race relations.

We all know that politicians speak in code.... In Britain in 1995, if the issue of immigration is raised, people know that race is what is really being talked about. It is dishonest of Conservative Members to pretend, when supporting this legislation, that their only motivation is to clear up a few administrative processes. They know full well, just as I have known all my life, that, whenever politicians raise the issue of immigration in public debate, it is always entangled with issues of race....

My party is united in opposing this legislation, and we shall oppose it tonight. It has nothing to do with the real administrative problems relating to illegal immigration. It is about making race an issue in the coming general election campaign. Conservative Members whose parents came here as economic refugees should be ashamed to go through the lobby in support of such legislation.

Mr Nirj Joseph Deva (Brentford and Isleworth):   **I am pleased to follow the speech by the Hon Member for Hackney North and Stoke Newington (Ms Abbott). She made an honest speech on behalf of the old Labour Party – a speech that reflected the true spirit of the Labour Party, whatever the new Labour Party might want....**

I speak as an immigrant myself: I am proud to be one. I am now proud to be British as well. Good race relations are paramount, not only to people who have recently settled here but to everyone in the wider community. In the recent past, it was clear that the French lacked firm and fair immigration controls; that resulted in Mr Le Pen and the fascist right gaining ascendancy. I do not want that to happen here, which is why it is so important that fair and firm immigration controls be effectively applied, and be seen to be so. That is why the Bill is so timely.

The Bill protects the interests of one particular group of whom we have heard not a word from Labour Members – those who are genuine asylum-seekers. Genuine asylum-seekers are stuck in a huge queue of those who are not genuine asylum-seekers. They are in a state of limbo. They are left hanging around and no consideration is given to their prosperity or their prospects....

The processing of asylum applications is not as it should be. My Right Hon and learned friend the Home Secretary has produced a Bill simply and effectively to make the backlog disappear so that genuine asylum seekers can be settled here happily and bogus ones returned.

It is clear that our procedures are being abused. It does not require a genius to work out that if only 4% of applications are upheld by independent adjudicators, 96% of applicants are abusing the system.

Last year there were 2,030 applications from India. Five were
granted asylum by independent adjudicators and 30 were given
Exceptional Leave to Remain.... There have been problems in
the Punjab since 1984 but recently circumstances have improved
immeasurably. Elections have been held and the Punjab is quietly
settling down. There are still problems in Kashmir, but India is
a vast country, and it is difficult to designate a country as unsafe
when one small province is experiencing political or human
rights problems....

Finally, I would welcome the proposal to criminalise racketeers.
I would like to go further. I would like all immigration advisors
in the United Kingdom to be licensed or at least self-regulated.
I deal with case after case of people who have been exploited
and ripped off by so-called immigration advisors. The Bill is
timely; it is effective, it is humane, and it is imperative. (*Hansard*,
1995-96, vol 268, pp 765-69).

These speeches are interesting in that they present immigration and asylum
as a moral, and not simply an administrative, issue. Diane Abbott suggests,
for example, that Conservative members should be "ashamed" to go into
the lobby. Other speakers, like the Liberal MP David Alton, went
considerably further in accusing the government of being "wicked",
"unChristian" and "immoral" (*Hansard*, 1995-96, vol 268, p 737).
Conservative MPs were, however, equally forthright, in their support for
the Bill. For Nirj Deva, the measures it contained were "timely, humane,
just and necessary", and it was the Labour Party which was "playing the
race card", and letting down the "genuine" asylum-seeker. Michael
Howard also took the moral high ground in his opening speech:

Some have suggested that this is an immoral Bill. I reject that
utterly. It is not immoral to protect our asylum procedures
against the current massive level of abuse. It is not immoral to
declare that, in our judgement, the conditions in some countries
do not give rise to a serious risk of persecution. It is not immoral
to protect employment opportunities for those entitled to live
and work here, and it is not immoral to combat racketeering.
(*Hansard*, 1995-96, vol 268, p 712).

Given the wide gulf between these different evaluations, it is, perhaps, unsurprising that speakers were often at cross-purposes in presenting evidence. Diane Abbott contrasted the relatively low numbers seeking asylum in Britain with the much larger numbers in Germany, and suggested that more could be accepted, without this threatening the "British way of life". Other speakers, however, used the sharp rise in asylum-seekers as evidence that this was a problem that had to be addressed, as a matter of urgency, by any government.

Deva's speech drew upon the fact that only 4% were granted asylum which, in his view, was simple proof that the majority of asylum-seekers were disguised economic migrants. Few Labour speakers challenged this statistic, and it is also interesting that no one in the debate produced figures, which are easily available from the Home Office, showing that few asylum-seekers are actually deported. This may be because Conservative MPs were anxious to give the impression that the government was 'tough' and 'effective' in addressing the problem of immigration. Labour MPs, by contrast, may have wished to avoid raising difficult issues, that might have further stirred up prejudice in the public[8].

Ultimately, as in many varieties of political debate, the same 'facts' could be interpreted in widely different ways. This is because supporters of each party had different assumptions about the causes of racial prejudice, and the purpose of immigration control. For Diane Abbott, and many Labour speakers, the Bill was yet another example of the Conservatives "playing the race card" prior to a general election. The language of 'swamping' was not used by Conservative speakers in this debate; but it had been used by Enoch Powell in 1968 (when it lost him his job on the Conservative front bench), and was also used by Margaret Thatcher in 1978. Abbott argued that the "real" concern of Conservative MPs in these debates was the "threat" posed by immigrants – whether these were economic migrants, or asylum-seekers – to "the British way of life". This threat was, in her view, "unquantified and exaggerated", but it could be used to win votes from sections of the public who resented immigrants. The administrative problems of the court-system were simply used as an "excuse" by the Conservatives to "play the race card".

For Nirj Joseph Deva and other Conservatives, on the other hand, "firm and fair" controls were necessary to maintain "good race relations". On this reading of recent British history, the race riots during the 1950s and 1960s, and the rise of the National Front during the 1970s, were the result of governments being perceived as 'soft' on immigration. Deva's contribution to this debate illustrates that it is possible for an Asian Member of Parliament to support immigration controls; and, indeed, it should be remembered that established ethnic communities have generally been opposed to fresh immigration that might damage their position in British society.

Proposals by pressure groups and academics

There has been little debate about asylum and immigration policy outside the House of Commons in recent years, although a number of proposals for change have been made by pressure groups, and academics[9]. Most of these accept the need for some kind of immigration control, but want to reform the appeals process, or feel that the United Kingdom can absorb larger numbers. There are, however, a small number of organisations, which have campaigned for more radical changes, and the abolition of all controls.

Proposals for changing the appeals process

A number of organisations advanced proposals for changing the appeals process during the passage of the 1996 Act, and were consulted by the Labour government during its 1997-98 review. These include Amnesty International, Justice, the Immigration Law Practitioners' Association and the London Office of the United Nations High Commissioner for Refugees.

Most of these groups want more resources to be spent on the appeals system, but are opposed to the removal of benefits from asylum-seekers, or discrimination against particular applicants, through measures like the 'white list'. Representatives from the London Office of the United Nations High Commissioner for Refugees have met officials from the Home Office in a series of private meetings. The UNHCR wants more resources to be spent on enforcement, and a simpler system of decision making, based on centralised databases, rather than the interpretation of case-law[10].

Academic studies have tended to accept the need for immigration controls, while suggesting that the present system could be made considerably fairer. Cohen (1994) wants there to be an independent determination process:

> **... given the evidence of abuse of power by civil servants and politicians in the case of asylum-seekers, there is a good case to**

> establish a quasi-independent Office for the Recognition,
> Protection, and Welfare of Refugees, along the lines of the French
> OFPRA. Since 1979, the main forms of abuse have been two:
> the immediate rush to legislation or judicial appeal whenever
> the courts have found against the actions of an official or a
> minister; and, second, the sense of an unscalable and united
> wall of [immigration officers], Home Office officials, police
> and media. Such agents and agencies should not be in sole
> charge of evaluating asylum claims. (Cohen, 1994, p 215)

A (1994) collection edited by Sarah Spencer for the Institute for Public
Policy Research also contains a long list of recommendations for changing
government policies towards immigration and asylum. One contribution,
which was written before the 1993 Asylum and Immigration Act, broadly
accepts the need for measures to deter asylum-seekers from arriving in
the United Kingdom (Randall, 1994). However, it also suggests that
more resources should be given to the Home Office in conducting the
initial interview. A more radical proposal is that Britain should give
more refugees Exceptional Leave to Remain, and cut down the resources
spent on determining refugee status under the Convention.

More radical proposals

The overall argument in Spencer's collection is that more needs to be
done, by Britain and other countries in the developed world, about the
causes of the refugee problem, rather than simply addressing the
symptoms[11]. She also suggests that we should recognise the economic
benefits of immigration, and, perhaps, adopt the approach of America
which selects immigrants on the basis of labour market needs. In any
event, a more rational policy would be preferable to the current haphazard,
and often unfair, procedures operated by the Home Office.

This can be contrasted to the more radical position, advanced in a
series of books, and pamphlets, by the Greater Manchester Immigration
Aid Unit over the last 20 years, in which immigration control is viewed
as a symptom of global economic inequalities, originally caused by Western
imperialism (Cohen, 1992, 1995). One publication asks, for example:

> ... why should people not be allowed to migrate for economic
> reasons? After all, western colonialists occupied, often personally,
> half the world for economic reasons. It is the consequences of

this economic history, a history which still continues today, that makes it impossible to distinguish 'political' from 'economic migrants'. For instance, the reason there has been migration to the UK from the Indian sub-continent, Africa and the Caribbean is because this country has destroyed the economy of those massive areas of the world through economic exploitation made possible by political power and military force. As the Asian Youth Movement used to say: 'We are here, because you were there'. (Cohen, 1995, p 35)

From this perspective, campaigns on behalf of individuals are ultimately self-defeating. Rejecting all controls is the only consistent position that can be taken if you believe that borders are unfair.

Immigration control and public opinion

Although there has been a great deal of political activity and debate about the plight of asylum-seekers in recent years, it should be remembered that most people have little interest in immigration control. This can be contrasted with the strong feelings about immigration that led thousands of people to support Enoch Powell in the 1970s, or return anti-immigration candidates in constituencies with a high immigrant presence. By contrast, those Conservatives who made immigration an issue in 1997 (most notably Nicholas Budgen in Wolverhampton) lost their seats, although the swing against them was no greater than in many other constituencies around the country. Asylum still raises passions in areas like Dover which receive large numbers of asylum-seekers, and right-wing newspapers like the *Daily Mail* continue to campaign vigorously for more controls. However, opinion polls suggest that the public is more concerned about other issues.

It is also arguable that asylum has generated relatively little opposition from liberals, who are more concerned about other areas of public policy, such as poverty or the environment. Attendance at meetings supporting asylum-seekers is generally disappointing. To give one example, eight people attended a public meeting in High Wycombe in early 1996, organised by the Campaign Against the Asylum Bill. The national demonstrations that have been held in London against the 1996 and 1999 Acts have attracted a few thousand people, but this can be contrasted to the much larger numbers who marched on the British National Party Head Quarters in 1993 when the issue was race, rather than immigration.

One civil servant in the Immigration and Nationality Department summarised the political climate surrounding immigration in the following terms:

I: Of all the areas I've been in, this is the one where the public in general are the least informed. I think it's a huge bluff, the way we operate. The general perception is that the government is tough on immigration. But, if you look at the figures, there's 40 or 50,000 people each year who come here illegally. We're removing about 4,000 each year. Now if this goes on for the next couple of years, you start to think....

In one sense, the government gets the worst of both worlds, because in certain quarters they are reasonably tough.... It only takes one Joy Gardiner case to create that perception, but that's just one case. There are many others where people just aren't being refused, but, on the other hand, the government wins by putting in relatively little resources. You know, if it's a Conservative government, they wish to be tough on immigration. They can have that perception without investing as many resources as some people might say you would need...

Because its the status quo, and because there's not much between anyone on this – I don't suppose there is in many areas now – this is not something the public jump up and down about. You can speak to the man in certain parts of the country, you know, the taxi drivers around Leeds, where they can tell you what an outrage it is, and all the benefits these people have. And then you've got your quite vocal people who think it's an outrage that we've cut off the benefits.... And, you know, one rule of government is that, if you're upsetting both sides [wry smile], you've got it about right.

MT: And the people in the middle, the vast majority?

I: Just don't know, or don't care, or both. I think people are not well-informed or interested in this area. I wasn't before I came here.

This detached assessment provides an example of the way in which many civil servants, and politicians in all political parties, have a professional interest in public opinion. During the 1970s, many more members of the public had strong views about immigration, which governments had to take seriously. Since the 1980s, there has, however, been relatively little pressure for governments to restrict the numbers entering the country through either immigration or asylum. In many respects, immigration is no longer a political issue.

Notes

[1] There is also no evidence to suggest that it was a crucial issue in the 1979 general election, which was mainly fought on the economic record of the Labour government, and its responsibility for widespread strikes that took place during the so-called 'winter of discontent'.

[2] For an entertaining account of the work of government ministers, see Kaufman (1997).

[3] There was an audience of about 40 people at the session I attended who were mainly representatives from the 30 or so pressure groups and associations who submitted evidence to the panel. See *Report of the Glidewell Panel* (1996).

[4] See Bolchover (1993) for an analysis of the role of communal leaders in the Jewish Community in attempting to influence British policy during the Second World War.

[5] There are about 800-1,000 asylum-seekers detained at any one time, out of an estimated 60,000 who are waiting for a decision from the Home Office, or for their appeals to be heard in the immigration courts. The relatively small number reflects the limited resources which have so far been available to the Home Office, who do not have the money to open new detention centres, or buy more places in prisons. From this point of view, the main purpose of detentions is to act as a deterrent. As one Presenting Officer told me, it was one way in which Britain could send out the message that "we are not a soft touch".

[6] The prosecution case collapsed during the trial in June 1998 when it became clear that staff were unable to identify the defendants on the CCTV videos taken inside the detention centre during the riot.

[7] This is partly a reference to Michael Howard, whose parents came to Britain as refugees in the 1930s.

[8] According to some informants, the Labour Party had deliberately chosen to respond to the Conservatives' attempt to 'play the race card' by adopting what politicians call a 'soft-bat' approach to the issue. The objective was to challenge government policy, without giving the impression that Labour were 'soft' on immigration.

[9] More public debate took place in the late 1960s and 1970s when a whole series of books and pamphlets were published about immigration control (for example, Steel, 1969, Moore and Wallace, 1975; see also Dummett, 1986). At present there appear to be only a handful of journalists who write regularly about this aspect of government policy.

[10] Two practical obstacles would make it difficult for any government to make radical changes to the appeals court-system. It would, to begin with, require a full-scale piece of legislation to repeal or substantially alter the 1971 Immigration Act, which would take up a lot of parliamentary time in any government programme. It would also be expensive setting up an entirely new system to determine refugee status.

[11] This seems to be a plea for sending more overseas aid to refugee producing countries, in the hope that it will reduce the numbers migrating to the West. In 1995, there were an estimated 13.2 million refugees in the world (and an additional 40 million 'displaced persons' within their own frontiers), so the 100,000 who applied for asylum in Europe represents only part of a much larger international problem (Mortimer, 1996). The current crisis in Kosovo has produced about half a million refugees.

Conclusion

Perhaps the most striking feature of the academic literature about immigration and asylum in Britain is the high moral tone it adopts towards the policies of successive governments. One of the first sociological accounts about the determination and appeals process was *Slamming the door* by Moore and Wallace (1975), which was written at a time when most people in the country, and all the main political parties favoured immigration controls. Moore and Wallace had no illusions that their findings – mainly case studies, based on interviews with Asians who had experienced ill-treatment at the hands of the immigration service and Entry Clearance Officers – would lead to any change in public opinion. Instead, they wanted their book to 'bear witness' to the experience of migrants excluded from Britain, and divided families, so that future, more enlightened, generations could know what had taken place in their name.

Academics today, both in Britain and internationally, continue to write despairingly about what they view as the wickedness of controls. One recent book review concludes with a plea for readers to listen to those who are putting forward recommendations for change:

> **If we do not listen, then we cannot console ourselves that we are merely marginalizing the words of academics. We will, in fact, be dismissing the agonies of others in the full knowledge of what we do, and in the words of George Lamming in *The emigrants*: to live comfortably with the enemy within you is the most criminal of betrayals. (Cheney, 1996, p 268)**

The editor of a journal that publishes 'progressive' or 'critical' research in discourse analysis invites contributions about this topic with a similar plea for academics to search their consciences:

> **Keeping our eyes, ears and mouths shut ... makes us directly responsible for, if not guilty of, the perpetuation of ethnic inequality and injustice. If we prevent ourselves, and our students, from critically examining the many discursive practices**

> involved, we tacitly side with those whose policies and public
> discourse indirectly cause or condone the beatings and raids by
> the police ... or the harassment by officials against the Others
> .... If discourse is prominently involved in producing this new
> Apartheid, we should be the experts to analyse and denounce
> it. If discourse analysts do not want to be part of such a solution,
> history will decide that they were part of the main problem of
> the twentieth century. (Van Dijk, 1996, p 292)

In contrast to this engaged, and unashamedly moralistic form of writing,
my own objective in this study has been to examine some aspects of
immigration control in Britain, including the character of political debates
about immigration, as a sociological topic. As I demonstrated in Chapter
One, there are a number of traditions in sociology, that can help us
understand the causes of migration, and its effects on British society.
Both the consensus tradition represented by Park, and the conflict tradition
represented by British Marxist, neo-Marxist and poststructuralist writers
offer ways of understanding racial and ethnic relations, which can be
used to make sense of immigration control. There is arguably a need for
more research on how immigrants adapt to British society, building on
the achievements of researchers from the late 1960s and early 1970s, and
perhaps re-examining Robert Park's ideas about the race-relations cycle.
There is also a continuing need for research on the political economy of
migration, and the role of legal and illegal immigrants in the economies
of Western countries. Although sociology is currently in a weakened
state, both intellectually and institutionally, as an academic discipline in
Britain, there continues to be a need for theoretically-informed research
about social processes that does more than offer a selective description of
the facts, interspersed with moral commentary.

My own contribution, as a sociologist working in the interpretive
tradition, has been to describe a range of institutional and practical
perspectives in the immigration courts. Given more time, I would have
liked to have gone further in addressing a wider range of perspectives.
More empirical research could, for example, be undertaken on the
perspective and experience of different appellants, on the civil service,
and on politicians. I am also conscious that a much larger study could
have looked in more detail at how the courts determine a wider range of
appeals, and the relationship between routine decision making by
adjudicators, and the development of immigration law in the higher courts.
Nevertheless, despite these omissions, I hope to have conveyed a sense of

how the immigration courts are viewed by legal practitioners, civil servants, politicians and appellants which goes beyond the usual stereotypes.

There has always been a recurring debate in sociology over whether the discipline should be 'political', or 'value-free', in the way it describes the social world (see, for example, Gouldner, 1962; Becker, 1967). In the more recent literature, in theoretically sophisticated sub-fields like the sociology of science and technology, this has become a debate about the merits of 'relativism' and 'essentialism' (Grint and Woolgar, 1997, Chapter 6). In relation to immigration control, a relativist would, presumably, treat all viewpoints as equivalent, whether these are for or against immigration controls, whereas an essentialist would want to defend an objective epistemological position which gives academics the right to advance moral and political arguments in the academy.

This debate goes back at least as far as the early years of this century when it was common for academics in German universities to promote their own political and moral views to students and the public. Max Weber argued that the role of the sociologist should not be to make value judgements about government policies. It is worth reproducing some comments which illustrate his distaste for moral advocacy by university academics:

> **Every teacher has observed that the faces of his students light up, and they become more attentive, when he begins to set forth his personal evaluations, and that the attendance at his lectures is greatly increased by the expectation that he will do so. Everyone knows furthermore that in the competition for students, universities in making recommendations for advancement, will often give a prophet, however minor, who can fill the lecture halls, the upper hand over a much superior scholar who does not present his own preferences. Of course, it is understood in those cases that the prophecy should leave sufficiently untouched the political or conventional preferences which are generally accepted at the time.... I regard all this as very undesirable.... For my own part, I fear that a lecturer who makes his lectures stimulating by the insertion of personal evaluations will, in the long run, weaken the students' taste for sober empirical analysis. (Weber, 1949, p 9)**

Political philosophers have often been far more sensitive than social scientists to the difficult moral choices that are involved in preventing or allowing movement across boundaries (for example, Walzer, 1983; Hoffman, 1981; see also Dillon, 1995). Weber might argue, however, that, in order to make moral judgements, it is necessary to face uncomfortable facts. Partisan accounts can hardly be avoided in political debate, but they usually put forward simplistic solutions, based on a morally-driven view of social reality. I hope that my account of how decisions are made in these courts, and the administrative problems they create for the civil service, will make it possible for politicians, and others, to think more critically about this area of policy.

Despite adopting a tough and uncompromising stance towards immigration, successive British governments have only had a limited success in preventing secondary immigration from the Indian subcontinent, and what is effectively a new wave of immigration by asylum-seekers since the late 1980s. The numbers who came over from Asia (many of them through the arranged marriage system) were quite large, in relation to the numbers who are now claiming asylum. Together, however, they represent a tiny proportion of the British population, and will be absorbed over time, culturally and biologically, into what remains a relatively homogeneous society. This is not to deny the increasingly multicultural nature of our larger cities, and the importance of combating racism, and changing the way we think about being British. It does, however, suggest that problems associated with immigration have been much smaller in Britain than in many countries around the world. The relatively consensual reaction to events like the racist murder of Stephen Lawrence should be compared with the regular riots that still take place in America, and European countries, about similar issues. The fate of the National Front in Britain can be contrasted with the success of extreme right-wing parties in France and Germany in winning seats in national elections.

Although it seems unlikely that appeals will be determined within a six-month period by 2001, one can predict that the system will become faster, and more asylum-seekers will be deported. There will be increasing cooperation between governments in the European Economic Community with the aim of preventing asylum-seekers from travelling to Europe. Some hope to establish a 'Fortress Europe', in which it will become more difficult to cross borders, and tough measures are taken to identify and remove illegal immigrants.

If one adopts a longer historical perspective, it seems inevitable that even greater numbers will be drawn to Europe in the 21st century, given the availability of cheap air fares, and the growing international divide between rich and poor. Deterrence measures such as putting asylum-seekers in detention centres, or withdrawing social security benefits, will have no long-term effect on people who are genuinely fleeing political persecution, or on many economic migrants. These are uncomfortable facts, which are seldom acknowledged or discussed by politicians. They suggest that the most honest policy we could pursue would be to accept those who do succeed in reaching these shores in a more generous, and tolerant, spirit.

Bibliography

Althusser, L. (1969) *For Marx*, London: New Left Books.

Anthias, F. and Yuval-Davis, N. (1992) *Racialised boundaries: Race, nation, colour, and class, and the anti-racist struggle*, London: Routledge.

Ashcroft, B., Griffiths, G. and Tiffin, H. (eds) (1995) *The post-colonial studies reader*, London: Routledge.

Atkinson, J.M. (1982) 'Understanding formality: the categorization and production of "formal" interaction', *British Journal of Sociology*, vol 33, no 1, pp 86-117.

Atkinson, J.M. and Drew, P. (1979) *Order in court: The organisation of verbal interaction in court settings*, London: Macmillan.

Back, L. (1996) *New ethnicities and urban culture: Racisms and multiculture in young lives*, London: UCL Press.

Baldwin, J. and McConville, M. (1977) *Negotiated justice: Pressures to plead guilty*, London: Martin Robertson.

Banks, M. (1996) *Ethnicity: Anthropological constructions*, London: Routledge.

Bannakar, R. (1997) 'The sociology of law: the child of an unholy marriage', Paper delivered at the *Annual Conference of the British Socio-Legal Studies Association*, University of Wales at Cardiff, April.

Banton, M. (1977) *The idea of race*, London: Tavistock.

Barbesino, P. and Singleton, A. (1995) 'The production and reproduction of knowledge on international migration in Europe', Paper presented to the *Conference on Nation and Migration in Southern Europe*, University of Greenwich, 18-20 December.

Becker, H. (1963) *Outsiders: Studies in the sociology of deviance,* New York, NY: The Free Press.

Becker, H. (1967) 'Whose side are we on?', *Social Problems*, vol 14, no 3, pp 237-48.

Becker, H., Hughes, E.C., Geer, G. and Strauss, A. (1961) *Boys in white*, Chicago, IL: University of Chicago Press.

Bevan,V. (1986) *The development of British immigration law*, London: Croom Helm.

Bhabha, H. (1994) *The location of culture*, London: Routledge.

Bhabha, J., Klug, F. and Shutter, S. (eds) (1985) *Worlds apart: Women under immigration and nationality law*, London: Pluto Press.

Blumberg, A. (1969) 'The practice of law as a confidence game', in A. Aubert (ed) *The sociology of law*, Harmondsworth: Penguin, pp 321-31.

Blumer, H. (1969) *Symbolic interactionism*, California, CA: University of California Press.

Bogardus, E.S. (1959) *Social distance*, Los Angeles, CA: Antioch Press.

Bolchover, R. (1993) *British Jewry and the Holocaust*, Cambridge: Cambridge University Press.

Bouvier, L. (1992) *Immigration and changing America*, New York, NY: Lanham.

Bradley, H. (1996) *Fractured identities: Changing patterns of inequality*, Cambridge: Polity Press.

Bulmer, M. and Solomos, J. (eds) (1999) *Ethnic and racial studies today*, London: Routledge.

Bunyan, T. (1991) 'Towards an authoritarian European State', *Race and Class*, vol 32, no 3, pp 15-28.

Calavita, K. (1992) *Inside the state: The Bracero Program, immigration and the INS*, New York, NY: Routledge.

Carlen, P. (1976) *Magistrates' justice*, Oxford: Martin Robertson.

Castles, S. and Kosack, C. (1973) *Immigrant workers and class structure in Western Europe*, Oxford: Oxford University Press.

Centre for Contemporary Cultural Studies (1982) *The empire strikes back: Race and racism in 1970s Britain*, London: Hutchinson.

Cheney, D. (1996) 'The never-never land of immigration, nationality and citizenship', *Journal of Law and Society*, vol 23, no 2, pp 263-8.

Cicourel, A.V. (1968) *The social organisation of juvenile justice*, New York, NY: Wiley.

Cicourel, A.V. and Kitsuse, J. (1963) *The educational decision makers*, New York, NY: Bobbs-Merrill.

Cohen, P. and Bains, H.S. (eds) (1988) *Multi-racist Britain*, London: Macmillan.

Cohen, R. (1994) *Frontiers of identity: The British and others*, Harlow: Longman.

Cohen, S. (1992) *Imagine there's no countries*, Manchester: Greater Manchester Immigration Aid Unit.

Cohen, S. (1995) *Still resisting after all these years: A century of international struggles against immigration controls 1895-1995*, Manchester: Greater Manchester Immigration Aid Unit.

Commission for Racial Equality (1985) *Immigration control procedures: Report of a formal investigation*, London: Commission for Racial Equality.

Conley, J.M. and O'Barr, W. (1998) *Just words: Law, language and power*, Chicago, IL: University of Chicago Press.

Cooley, C. (1918) *Social process*, Carbondale and Edwardsville, IL: Southern Illinois University Press.

Cornell, S. and Hartmann, D. (1997) *Ethnicity and race: Making identities in a changing world*, Thousand Oaks, CA: Pine Forge Press.

Dillon, M. (1995) 'Sovereignty and governmentality: from the problematics of the "New World Order" to the ethical problematic of the World Order', *Alternatives*, vol 20, pp 323-68.

Donald, J. and Rattansi, A. (1992) *'Race', culture and difference*, London: Sage Publications.

Drew, P. and Heritage, J. (eds) (1992) *Talk at work: Interaction in institutional settings*, Cambridge: Cambridge University Press.

Driedger, L. (1996) *Multi-ethnic Canada: Identities and inequalities*, Toronto, Canada: Oxford University Press.

Dummett, A. (1986) *Towards a just immigration policy*, London: Cobden.

Dummett, A. and Nicol, A. (1990) *Subjects, citizens and others: Nationality and immigration law*, London: Weidenfeld and Nicolson.

Emerson, R. (1969) *Judging delinquents: Context and process in juvenile court*, Chicago, IL: Aldine.

Faris, R. (1948) *Social disorganisation*, New York, NY: The Ronald Press.

Feeley, M. (1979) *The process is the punishment: Handling cases in a lower criminal court*, New York, NY: Russell Sage Foundation.

Fitz, J. and Halpin, D. (1994) 'Ministers and mandarins: educational research in elite settings', in G. Walford (ed) *Researching the powerful in education*, London: UCL Press.

Frazier, E.F. (1957) *Black bourgeoisie*, Glencoe, IL: The Free Press.

Gartner, L. (1960) *The Jewish immigrant in England 1870-1914*, London: Allen and Unwin.

Genn, H. and Genn, Y. (1983) *The effectiveness of representation at tribunals: Report to The Lord Chancellor*, London: Faculty of Laws, Queen Mary and Westfield College.

Giddens, A. (1990) *The consequences of modernity*, Cambridge: Polity Press.

Gilboy, J.A. (1991) 'Deciding who gets in: decision making by immigration inspectors', *Law and Society Review*, vol 25, no 3, pp 571-99.

Gilroy, P. (1987) *There ain't no black in the Union Jack: The cultural politics of race and nation*, London: Hutchinson.

Glass, R. (1960) *Newcomers: The West Indians in London*, London: Centre for Urban Studies.

Gouldner, A. (1962) 'Anti-minatour: the myth of a value-free sociology', *Social Problems*, vol 9, no 3, pp 199-212.

Grint, K. and Woolgar, S. (1997) *The machine at work: Technology, work and organization*, Cambridge: Polity Press.

Gusfield, J. (1966) *Symbolic crusade: Status politics and the American temperance movement*, Illinois, IL: Illinois University Press.

Hall, S. (1989) 'New ethnicities', in *Black film, British cinema*, ICA Documents 7, London: Institute of Contemporary Arts.

Hammersley, M. (1997) 'Qualitative data archiving: some reflections on its prospects and problems', *Sociology*, vol 31, no 1, pp 131-42.

Harvey, A. (1996) *The risks of getting it wrong: The Asylum and Immigration Bill Session 1995/6 and the determinations of special adjudicators*, London: Asylum Rights Campaign.

Hechter, M. (1987) *Principles of group solidarity*, California, CA: University of California Press.

Hennessy, P. (1989) *Whitehall*, London: Secker and Warburg.

Heritage, J. (1984) *Garfinkel and ethnomethodology*, Cambridge: Polity Press.

Hester, S. and Eglin, P. (1992) *A sociology of crime*, London: Routledge.

Hoffman, S. (1981) *Duties beyond borders*, Syracuse, NY: Syracuse University Press.

Holdaway, S. (1983) *Inside the British police: A force at work*, Oxford: Basil Blackwell.

Holmes, C. (1991) *A tolerant country? Immigrants, refugees and minorities in Britain*, London: Faber & Faber.

Home Office (1998) *Fairer, faster and firmer – A modern approach to immigration and asylum*, London: HMSO.

Hood, R. (1992) *Race and sentencing: A study in the Crown Court*, Oxford: Clarendon Press.

Hughes, E.C. (1994) *On work, race and the sociological imagination*, Chicago, IL: University of Chicago Press.

Hughes, E.C. and Hughes, H.C. (1981) 'What's in a name', *Where peoples meet*, Westport, CT: Greenwood Publishers.

Jagmohan, J. (1996) *The Short-Procedure: An analysis of the Home Office scheme for rapid initial decisions in asylum cases*, London: Asylum Rights Campaign.

Joly, D. and Cohen, R. (eds) (1989) *Reluctant hosts: Europe and its refugees*, Aldershot: Avebury.

Joly, D. with Kelly, L. and Nettleton, C. (1996) *Refugees in Europe: The hostile new agenda*, London: Minority Rights Group.

Juss, S. (1993) *Immigration, nationality and citizenship*, London: Mansell.

Katz, J. (1982) *Poor people's lawyers in transition*, New Brunswick, NJ: Rutgers University Press.

Kaufman, G. (1997) *How to be a Minister*, London: Faber & Faber.

Komter, M. (1997) 'Remorse, redress, and reform: blame-taking in the courtroom', in M. Travers and J. Manzo (eds) *Law in action: Ethnomethodological and conversation analytic approaches to law*, Aldershot: Ashgate, pp 241-66.

Lal, B. (1990) *The romance of culture in an urban civilisation: Robert E. Park on race and ethnic relations in cities*, London: Routledge.

Lash, S. and Urry, J. (1987) *The end of organised capitalism*, Cambridge: Polity Press.

Lash, S. and Urry, J. (1993) *Economies of signs and space*, London: Sage Publications.

Law, I. (1996) *Racism, ethnicity and social policy*, London: Prentice-Hall.

Layton-Henry, Z. (1984) *The politics of race in Britain*, London: Allen and Unwin.

Levi, J. and Walker, A. (eds) (1990) *Language in the judicial process*, New York, NY: Plenum.

Liebow, E. (1967) *Tally's corner: A study of negro streetcorner men*, Boston, MA: Little Brown.

Lipsky, M. (1980) *Street-level bureaucracy: Dilemmas of the individual in public services*, New York, NY: Russell Sage Foundation.

Lynch, M. (1993) *Scientific practice and ordinary action: Ethnomethodology and social studies of science*, Cambridge: Cambridge University Press.

Lynch, M. (1997) 'Preliminary notes on judges' work: the judge as a constituent of courtroom hearings', in M. Travers and J. Manzo (eds) *Law in action: Ethnomethodological and conversation analytic approaches to law*, Aldershot: Ashgate, pp 99-132.

McBarnet, D.J. (1981) *Conviction: Law, the state and the construction of justice*, London: Macmillan.

MacDonald, I. (1987) *Immigration law and practice*, 2nd edn, London: Butterworths.

MacDonald, I. and Blake, N. (1995) *Immigration law and practice*, London: Butterworths.

Mann, K. (1985) *Defending white collar crime: A portrait of attorneys at work*, New Haven, MA: Yale University Press.

Mason, D. (1990) 'A rose by any other name...? Categorisation, identity and social science', *New Community*, vol 17, no 1, pp 123-33.

Matoesian, G. (1993) *Reproducing rape*, Cambridge: Polity Press.

Matoesian, G. (1997) '"I'm sorry we had to meet under these circumstances": verbal artistry (and wizardry) in the Kennedy Smith Rape Trial', in M. Travers and J. Manzo (eds) *Law in action: Ethnomethodological and conversation analytic approaches to law*, Aldershot: Ashgate, pp 137-82.

Merton, R. (1976) 'Discrimination and the American creed', *Sociological ambivalence*, New York, NY: The Free Press, pp 190-221.

Miles, R. (1989) *Racism*, London: Routledge.

Miles, R. (1993) *Racism after 'race relations'*, London: Routledge.

Mills, H. (1996) 'Refugees to camp in shadow of scrubs', *The Observer*, 13 October.

Modood, T. (1992) *Not easy being British: Colour, culture and citizenship*, Stoke on Trent: Runnymede Trust and Trentham Books.

Moore, R. and Wallace, T. (1975) *Slamming the door: The administration of immigration control*, London: Robertson.

Morley, D. and Chen, K. (1996) *Stuart Hall: Critical dialogues in cultural studies*, London: Routledge.

Mortimer, E. (1996) 'The future of asylum in Europe', *Keynote Paper*, London: Refugee Legal Centre/UNHCR.

Myrdal, G. (1944) *An American dilemma: The Negro problem and modern democracy*, 2nd edn, New York, NY: Harper.

O'Barr, W.M. (1982) *Linguistic evidence: Language, power and strategy in the courtroom*, New York, NY: Academic Press.

OPCS (Office of Population Censuses and Surveys) (1991) *Census County Monitor 1991: Great Britain*, London: OPCS.

Pannick, D. with Blake, N., Persaud, S., Rose, D., Shaw, M. and Singh, R. (1993) *The primary purpose rule: A rule with no purpose*, London: Justice.

Park, R. (1939) 'The nature of race relations', in E.T.Thompson (ed) *Race relations and the race problem*, Durham, NC: Duke University Press, pp 3-45.

Paterson, A. (1982) *The Law Lords*, London: Macmillan.

Patterson, S. (1965) *Dark strangers: A sociological study of the absorption of a recent West Indian migrant group in Brixton, South London*, Harmondsworth: Penguin.

Peay, J. (1989) *Tribunals on trial: A study of decision making under the 1983 Mental Health Act*, Oxford: Clarendon Press.

Persons, S. (1987) *Ethnic studies at Chicago 1905-1943*, Urbana, IL: University of Illinois Press.

Plummer, K. (1983) *Documents of life: An introduction to the problems and literature of a humanistic method*, London: Unwin Hyman.

Pollins, H. (1989) *Hopeful travellers: Jewish migrants and settlers in nineteenth century Britain*, London: London Museum of Jewish Life.

Pollner, M. (1974) 'Explicative transactions: making and managing meaning in traffic court', in G. Psathas (ed) *Everyday language: Studies in ethnomethodology*, New York, NY: Irvington, pp 227-56.

Poulantzas, N. (1975) *Classes in contemporary capitalism*, London: New Left Books.

Prus, R. (1996) *Symbolic interaction and ethnographic research: Intersubjectivity and the study of human lived experience*, New York, NY: State University of New York Press.

Prus, R. (1997) *Subcultural mosaics and intersubjective realities: An ethnographic research agenda for pragmatizing the social sciences*, New York, NY: State University of New York Press.

Randall, C. (1994) 'An asylum policy for the UK', in S. Spencer (ed) *Strangers and citizens: A positive approach to migrants and refugees*, London: Rivers Oram Press, pp 202–31.

Rattansi, A. (1994) '"Western" racisms, ethnicities and identities in a "postmodern" frame', in A. Rattansi and S. Westwood (eds) *Racism, modernity and identity: On the Western Front*, Cambridge: Polity Press, pp 15-86.

Report of the Committee on Immigration Appeals (the Wilson Report) (1967) Cmnd 3387.

Report of the Franks Committee (1957) Cmnd 4060.

Report of the Glidewell Panel: An Independant Enquiry into the Implications and Effects of the Asylum and Immigration Bill 1995, and Related Social Security Measures (1996) London: Asylum Rights Campaign.

Report by Peat Marwick KPMG for the Home Office and Lord Chancellor's Department on Asylum Appeals Procedure (1994) London: KPMG.

Report of the Social Security Committee of the House of Commons on Benefits for Asylum Seekers (1996) London: HMSO.

Rock, P. (1986) A view from the shadows: The Ministry of the Solicitor-General of Canada and the making of the Justice for Victims of Crime Initiative, Oxford: Clarendon Press.

Rock, P. (1993) The social world of an English Crown Court: Witness and professionals in the Crown Court Centre at Wood Green, Oxford: Clarendon Press.

Rock, P. (1994) 'The social organisation of a Home Office initiative', European Journal of Crime, Criminal Law and Criminal Justice, vol 2, no 2, pp 141-67.

Rock, P. (1995) 'The opening stages of criminal justice policymaking', The British Journal of Criminology, vol 35, no 1, pp 1-16.

Sachdeva, S. (1993) The primary purpose rule in British immigration law, London: Trentham Books.

Saggar, S. (1992) Race and politics in Britain, London: Havester Wheatsheaf.

Said, E. (1991) Orientalism: Western conceptions of the Orient, Harmondsworth: Penguin.

Schutz, A. (1973) Collected papers, The Hague: Nijhoff.

Selznik, P. (1966) TVA and the grass roots: A study in the sociology of a formal organisation, New York, NY: Harper.

Sharrock, W.W. and Anderson, R.J. (1986) The ethnomethodologists, Chichester: Ellis Horwood.

Sivanandan, A. (1982) 'Race, class and the state', in A. Sivanandan, *A different hunger: Writings on black resistance*, London: Pluto, pp 101-25.

Skellington, R. (1996) *'Race' in Britain today*, 2nd edn, London: Sage Publications.

Smith, D. (1979) *The everyday world as problematic*, Milton Keynes: Open University Press.

Smith, P. (1992) *Immigration law practice and the Green Form Scheme: Report for the Immigration Law Sub-Committee of the Law Society*, London: The Law Society.

Smithies, B. and Fiddick, P. (eds) (1969) *Enoch Powell on immigration*, London: Sphere Books.

Solomos, J. (1986) 'Varieties of Marxist conceptions of "race", class and the state: a critical analysis', in J. Rex and D. Mason (eds) *Theories of race and ethnic relations*, Cambridge: Cambridge University Press, pp 84-109.

Solomos, J. and Back, L. (1996) *Racism and society*, Basingstoke: Macmillan.

Sorokin, P. (1956) *Fads and foibles in modern sociology and related sciences*, Chicago, IL: Regnery.

Spencer, I.R. (1997) *British immigration policy since 1939: The making of multi-racial Britain*, London: Routledge.

Spencer, S. (ed) (1994) *Strangers and citizens: A positive approach to migrants and refugees*, London: Rivers Oram Press.

Spivak, G.C. (1987) *In other worlds: Essays in cultural politics*, London: Methuen.

Steel, D. (1969) *No entry: The background and implications of the Commonwealth Immigrants Act*, London: Hurst.

The Stephen Lawrence Inquiry: Report of an Inquiry by Sir William Macpherson (1999) London: HMSO.

Sudnow, D. (1965) 'Normal crimes: sociological features of the penal code in a public defender office', *Social Problems*, vol 12, no 3, pp 255-76.

Thomas, W.I. and Znaniecki, F. (1958) *The Polish peasant in Europe and America*, New York, NY: Dover Publications (original editions published 1918-20).

Travers, M. (1996) 'Studying law-in-action: the case of the British immigration courts', Paper presented at the *Joint Meetings of the Law and Society Association and the Research Committee on Sociology of Law of the International Sociological Association*, University of Strathclyde, Glasgow, July.

Travers, M. (1997a) 'Preaching to the converted? Improving the persuasiveness of criminal justice research', *British Journal of Criminology*, vol 37, no 3, pp 359-77.

Travers, M. (1997b) *The reality of law: Work and talk in a firm of criminal lawyers*, Aldershot: Ashgate.

Tuitt, P. (1996) *False images: The law's construction of the refugee*, London: Pluto Press.

Van den Berghe, P.L. (1981) *The ethnic phenomenon*, New York, NY: Elsevier Press.

Van Dijk, T. (1996) 'Illegal aliens', *Discourse and Society*, vol 7, no 3, pp 291-2.

Wacker, R. (1995) 'The sociology of race and ethnicity in the second Chicago school', in G. Fine (ed) *A second Chicago school? The development of a postwar American sociology*, Chicago, IL: University of Chicago Press, pp 136-63.

Walford, G. (ed) (1994) *Researching the powerful in education*, London: UCL Press.

Walzer, M. (1983) *Spheres of justice: A defence of pluralism and equality*, Oxford: Basil Blackwell.

Webber, F. (1993) 'The new Europe: immigration and asylum', in T. Bunyan (ed) *State watching the new Europe: A handbook on the European state*, Nottingham: State Watch.

Weber, M. (1949) *The methodology of the social sciences*, New York, NY: The Free Press.

Weber, M. (1979) *Economy and society: An outline of interpretive sociology*, Berkeley, CA: University of California Press.

Young, C. (1996) 'Political representations of geography and place in the UK Asylum and Immigration Bill (1995)', Paper presented at the *Joint Meetings of the Law and Society Association and the Research Committee on Sociology of Law of the International Sociological Association*, University of Strathclyde, Glasgow, July.

Young, R. (1990) 'The effect of representation at tribunals', *CJQ*, 9 January, pp 16-23.

Index